50 MANDALA

Coloring Book For Adult Relaxtion

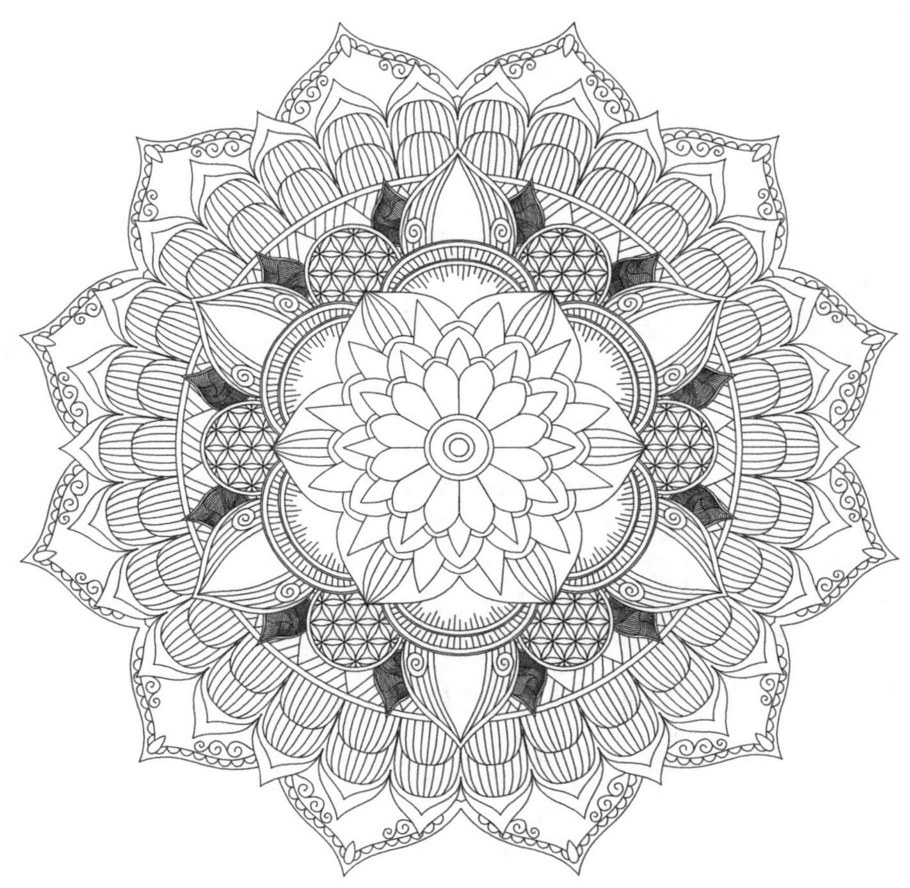

FLORAL BOOK

♥ GRAPHIC DESIGN STUDIO ♥

This Book Belongs To:

Color Test Page

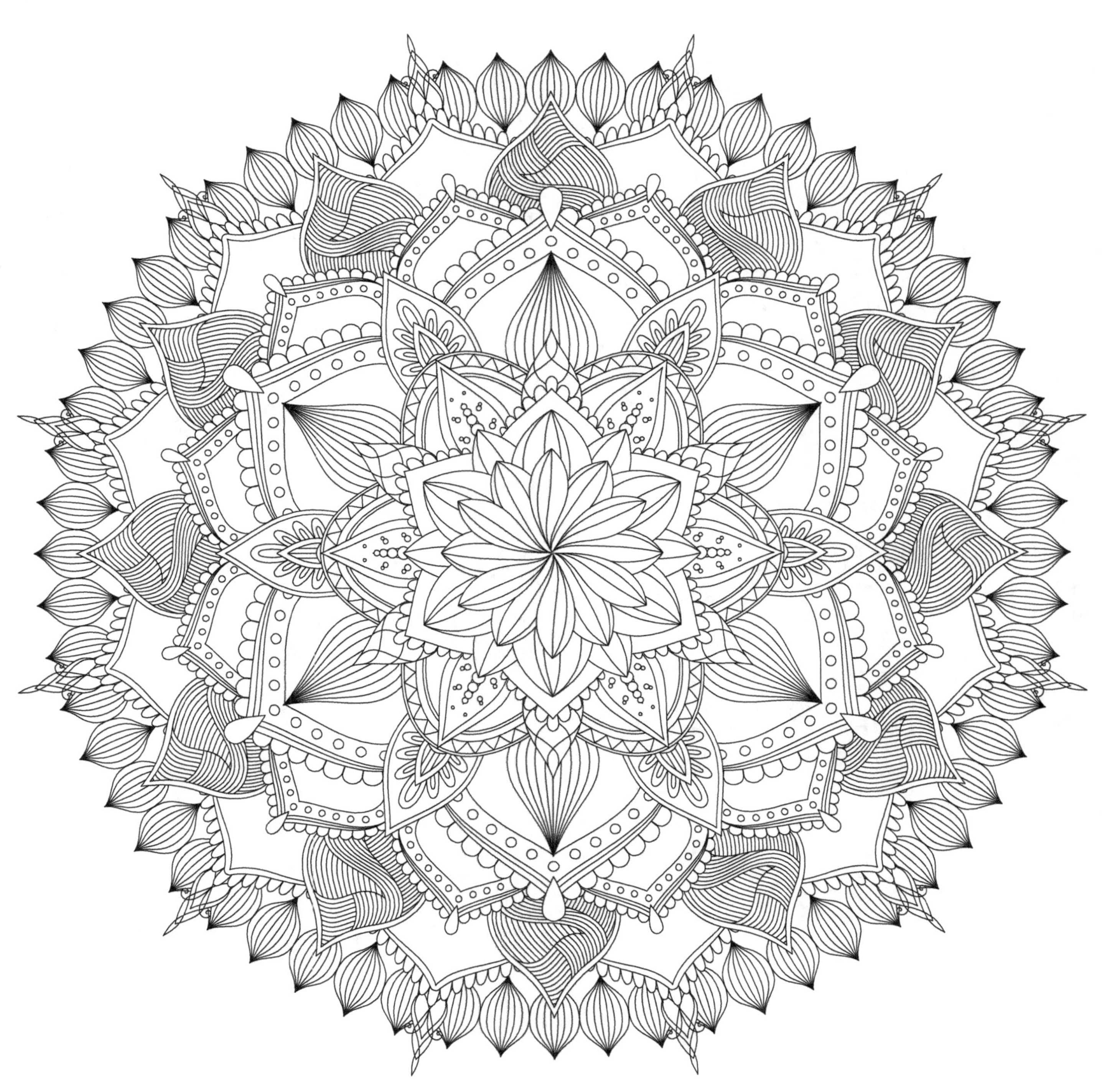

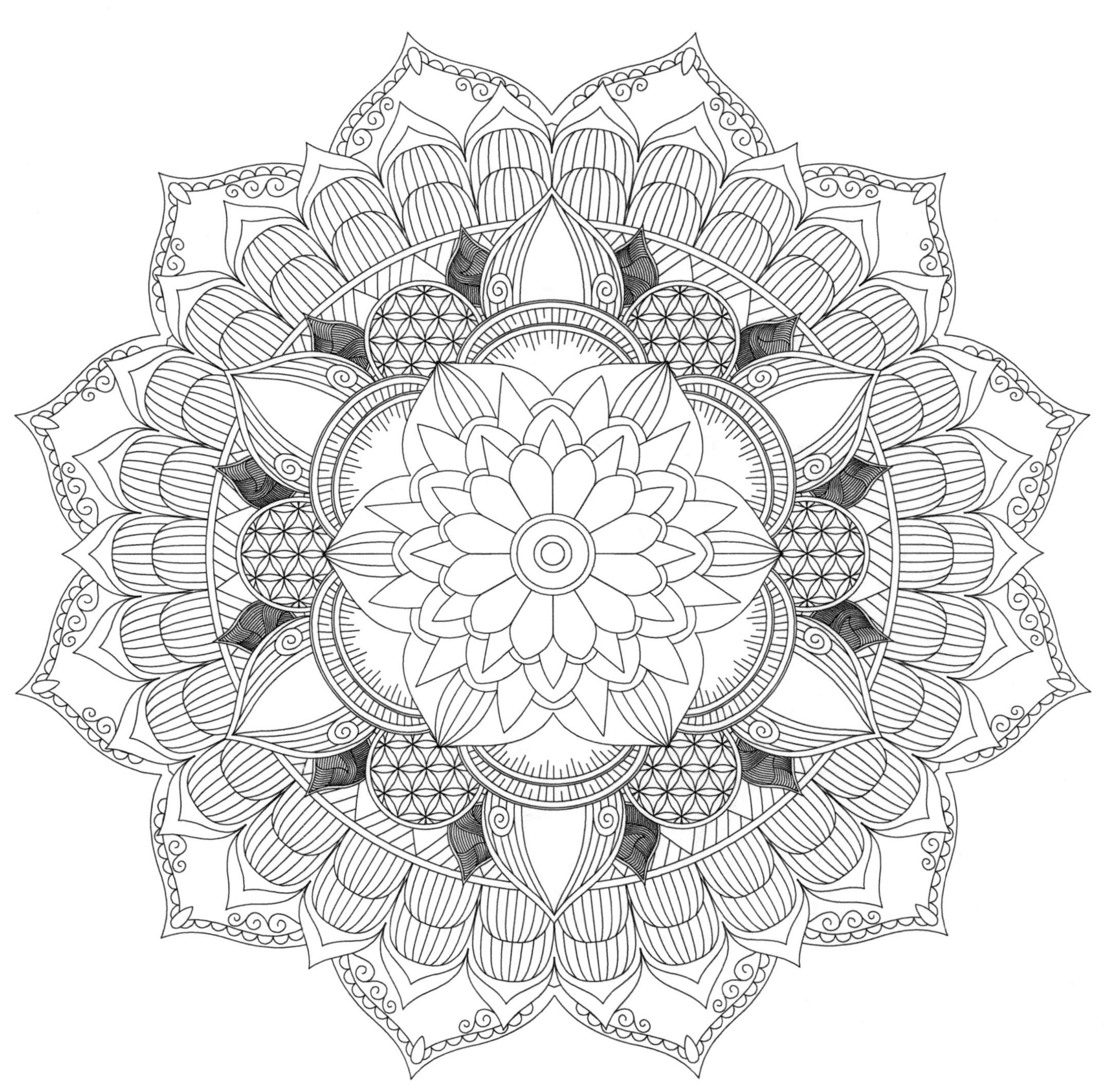

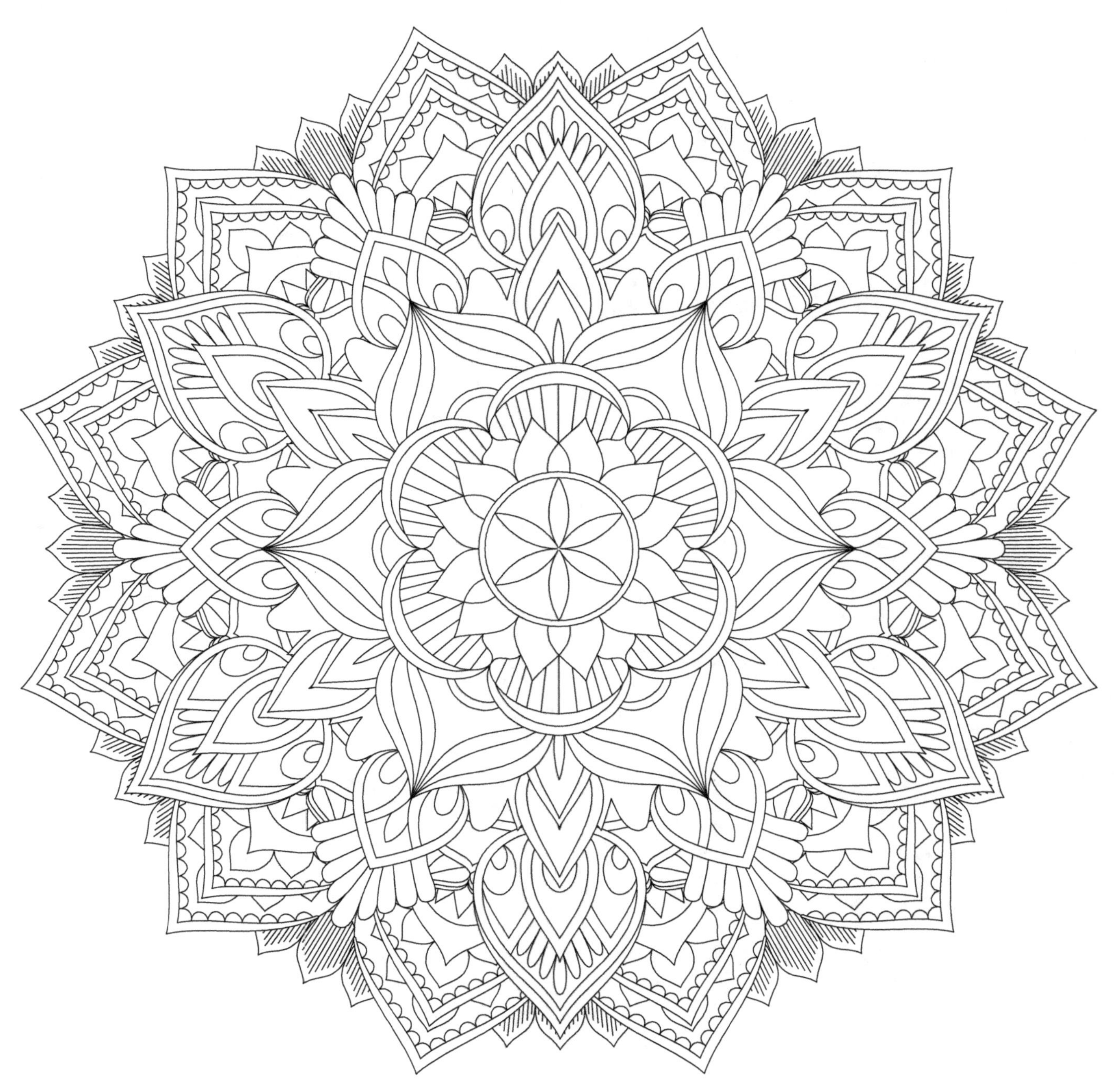

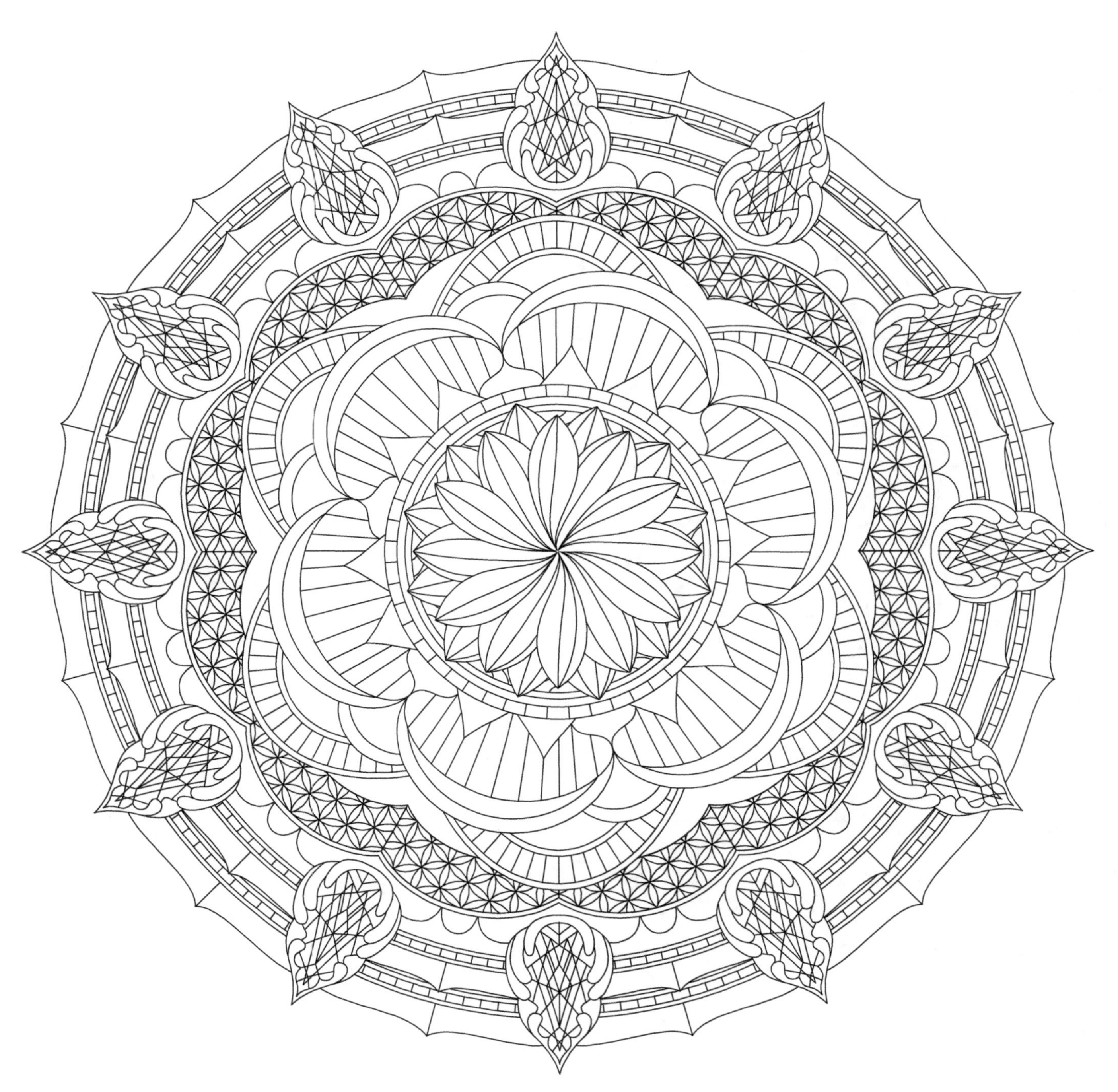

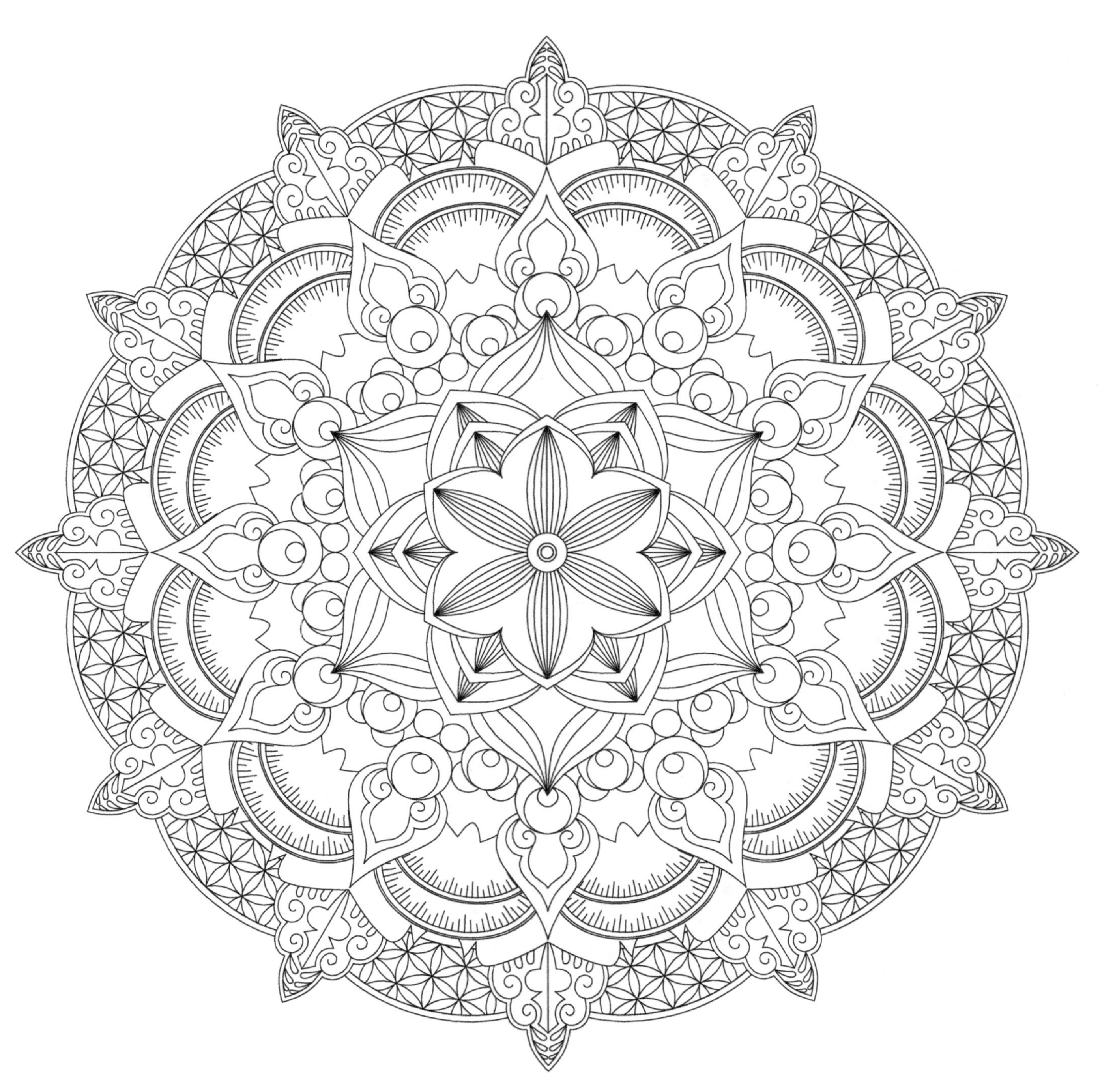

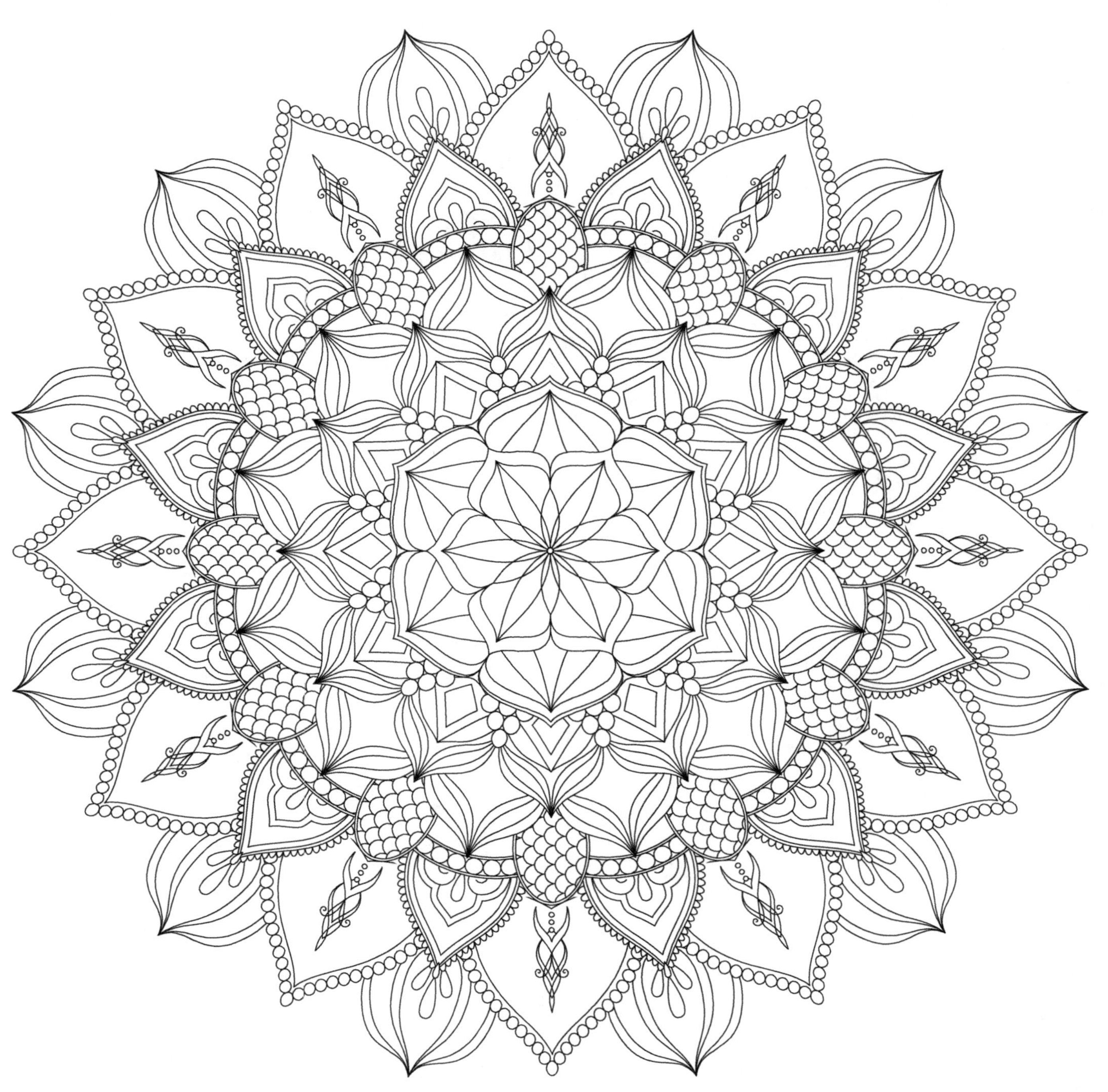

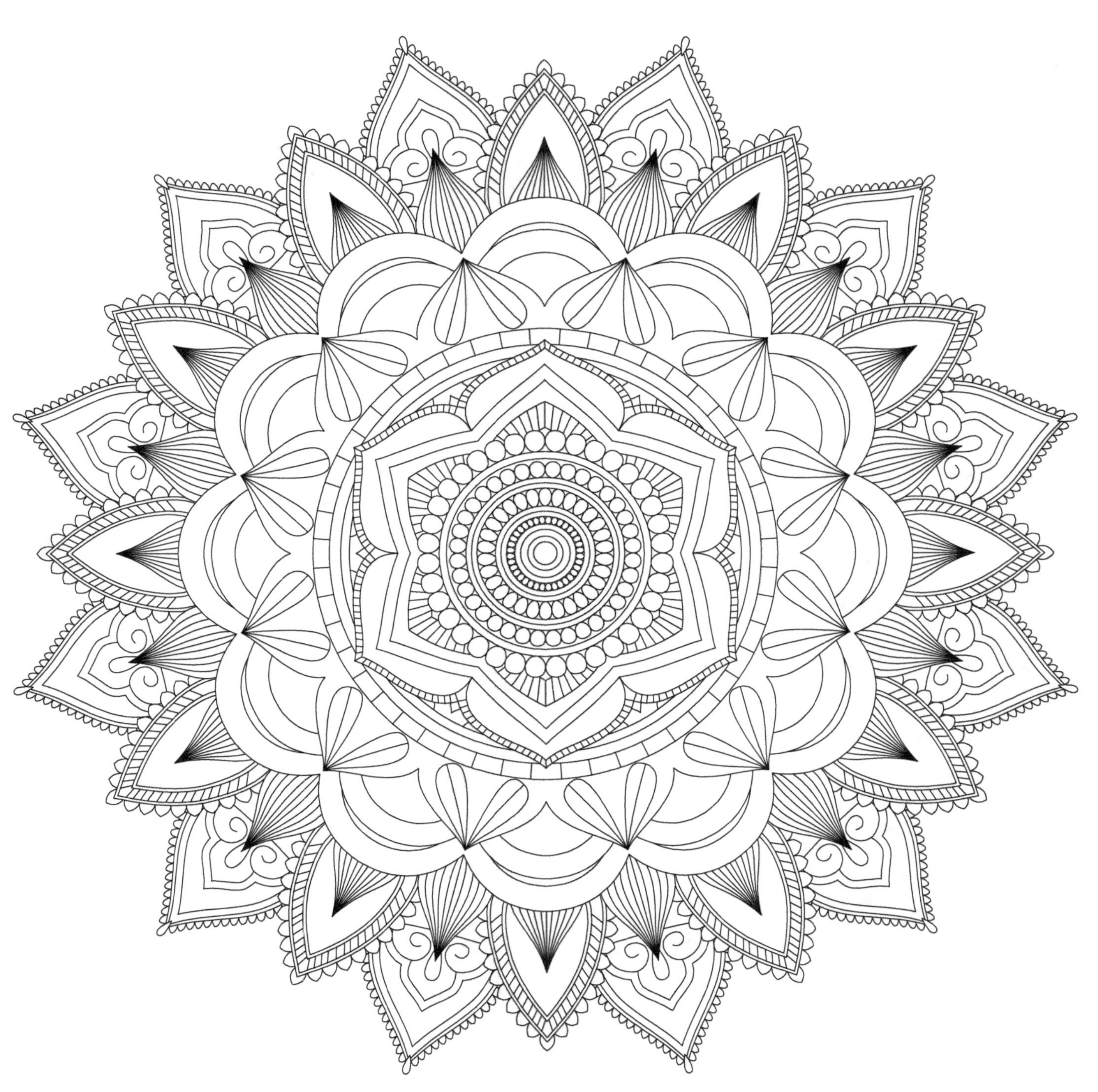

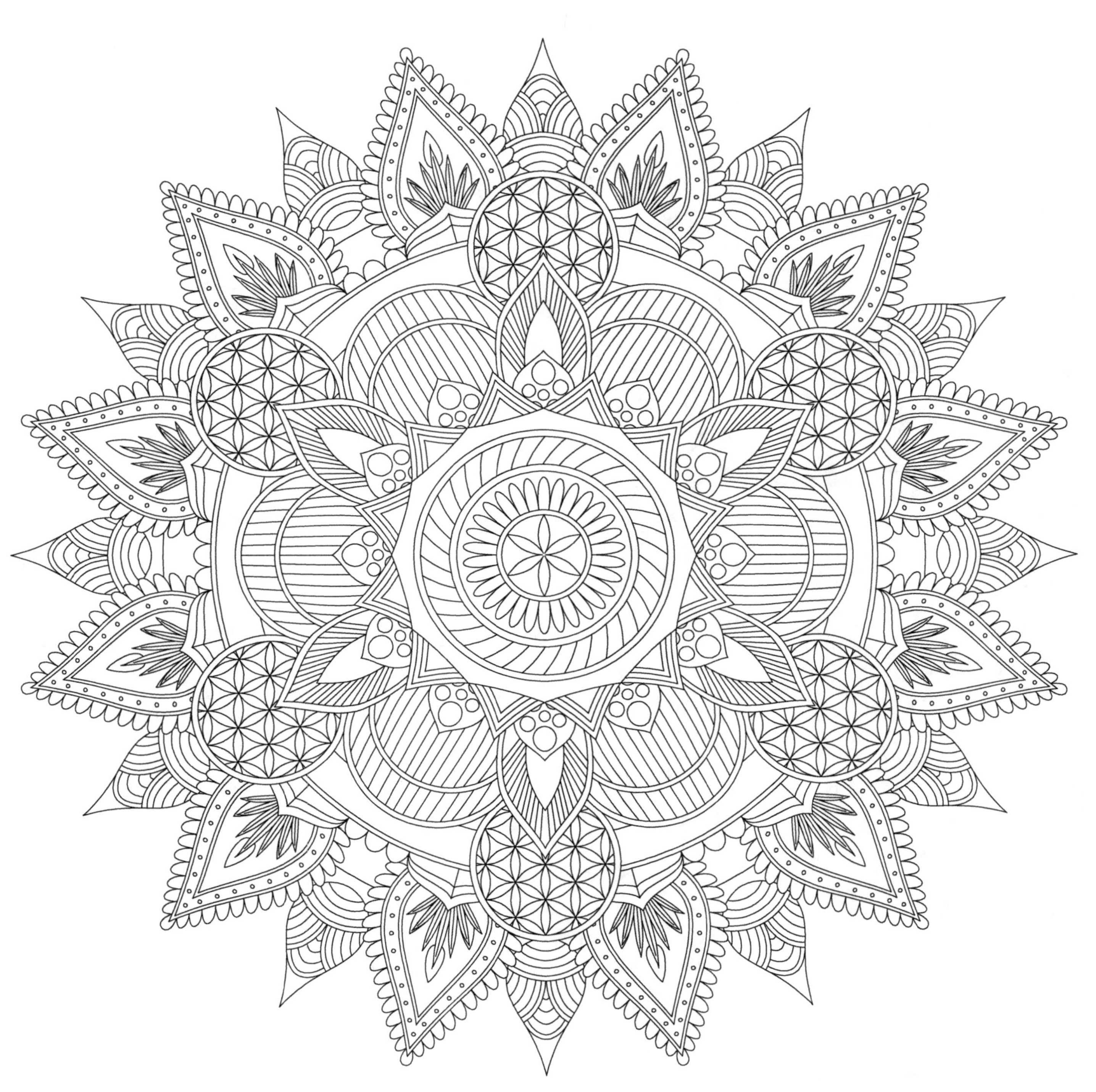

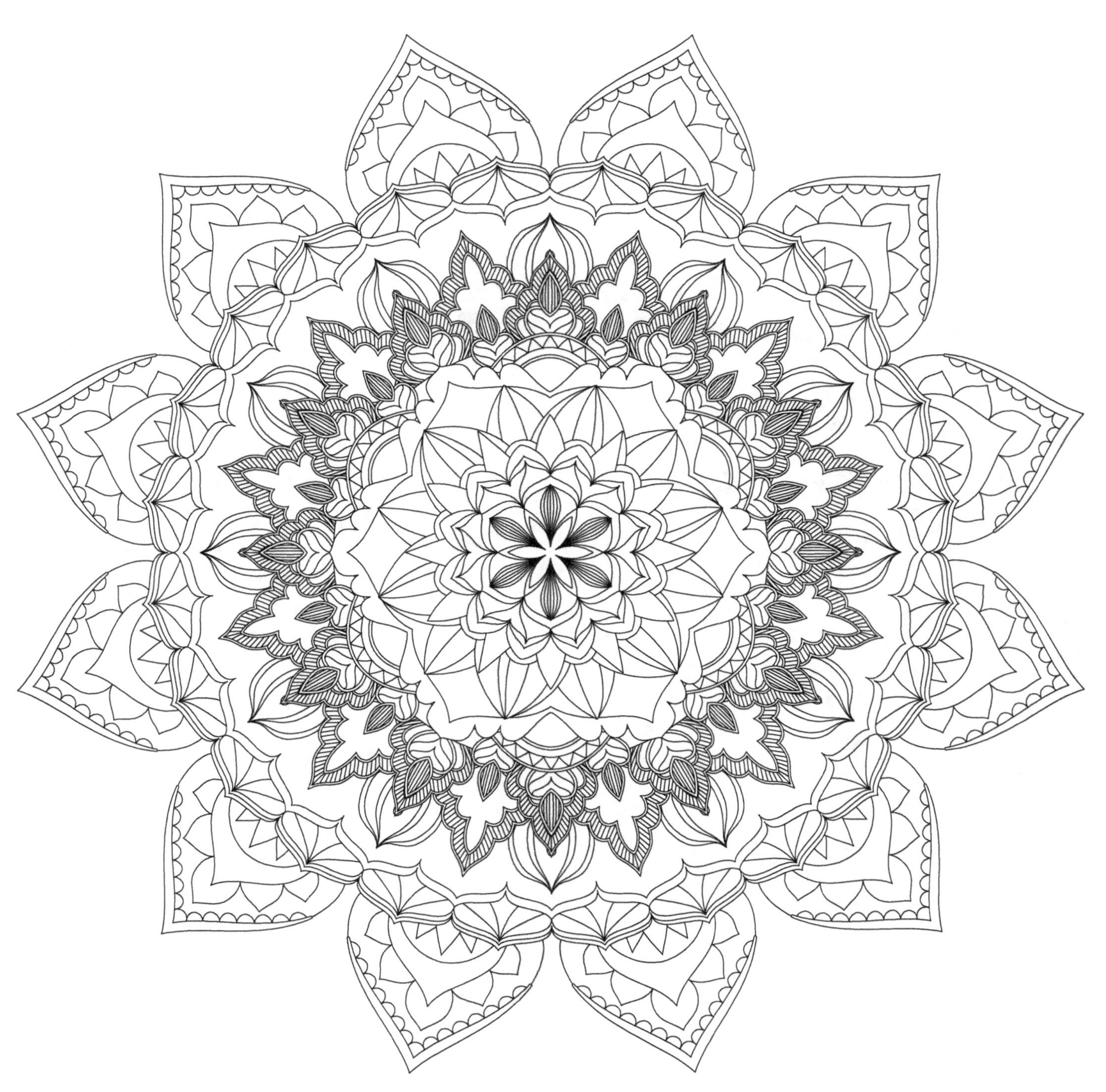

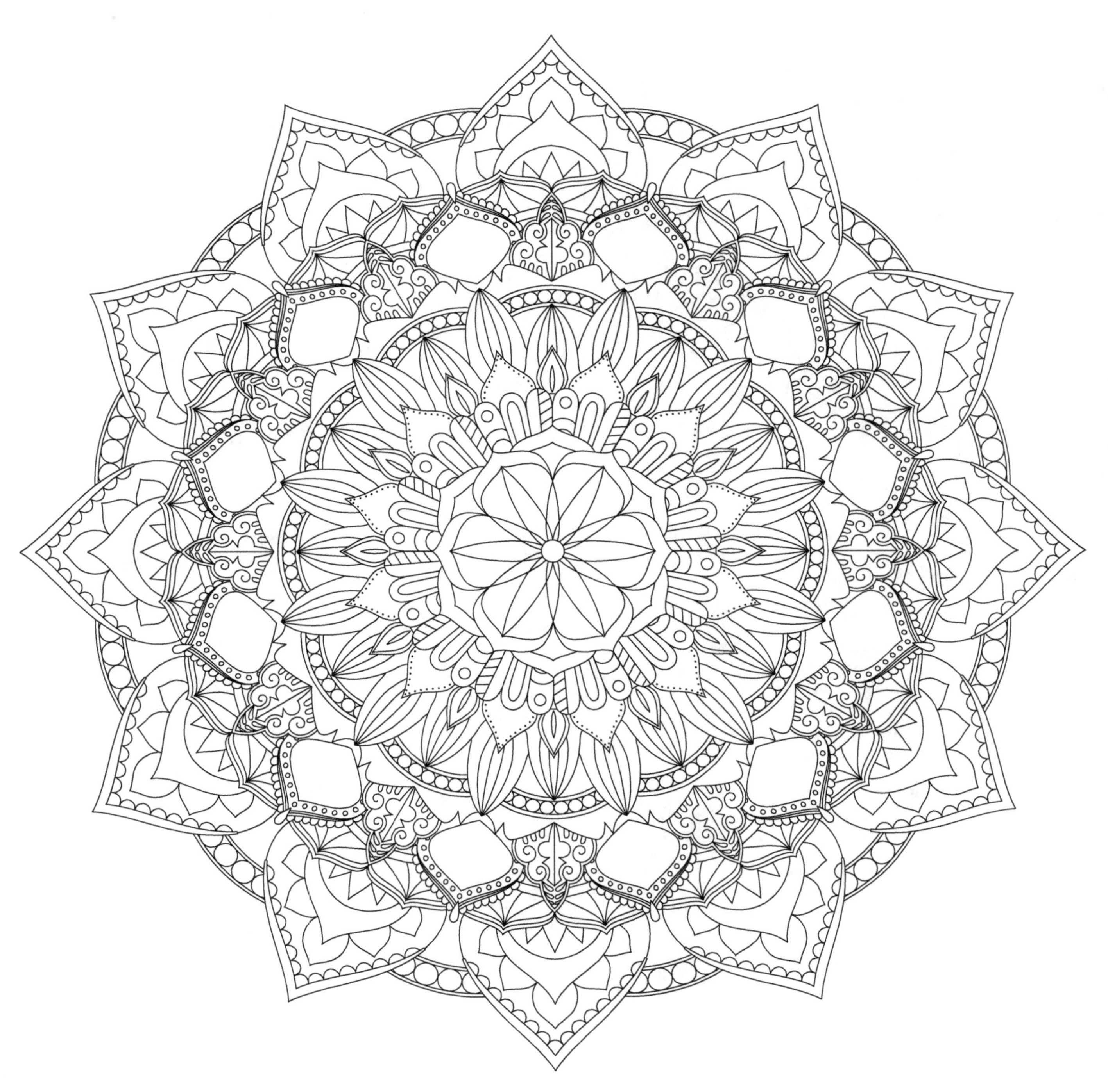

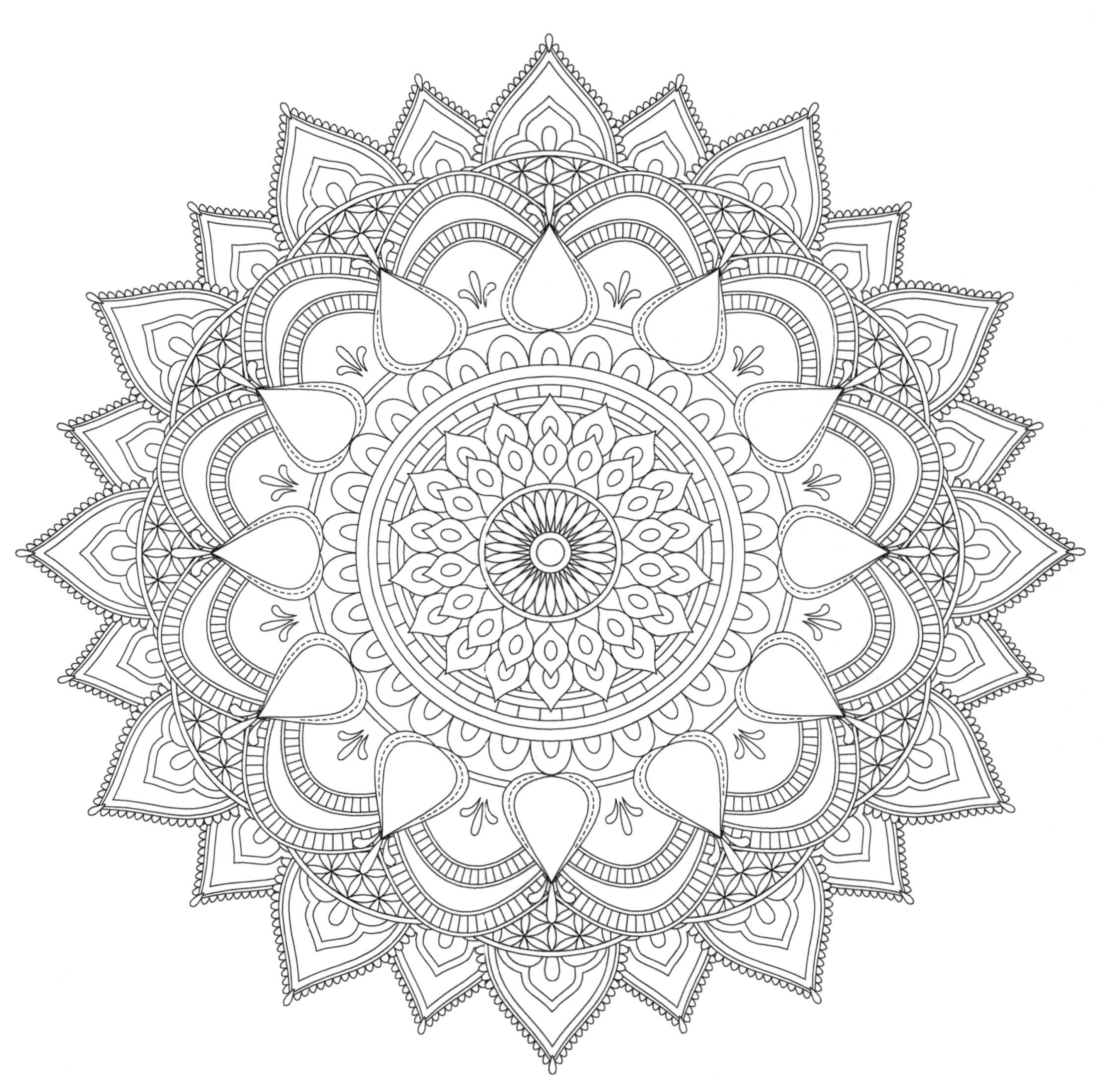

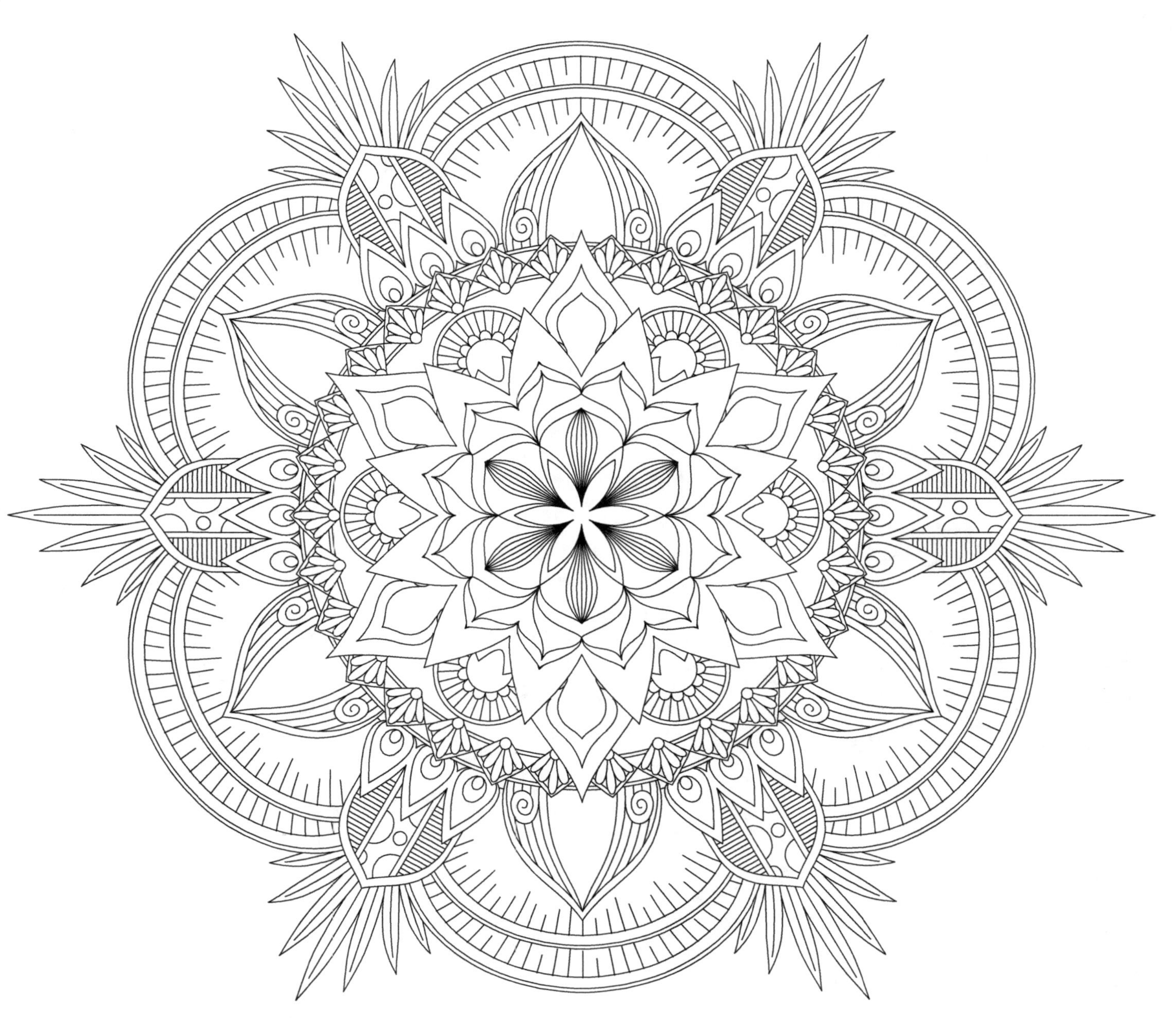

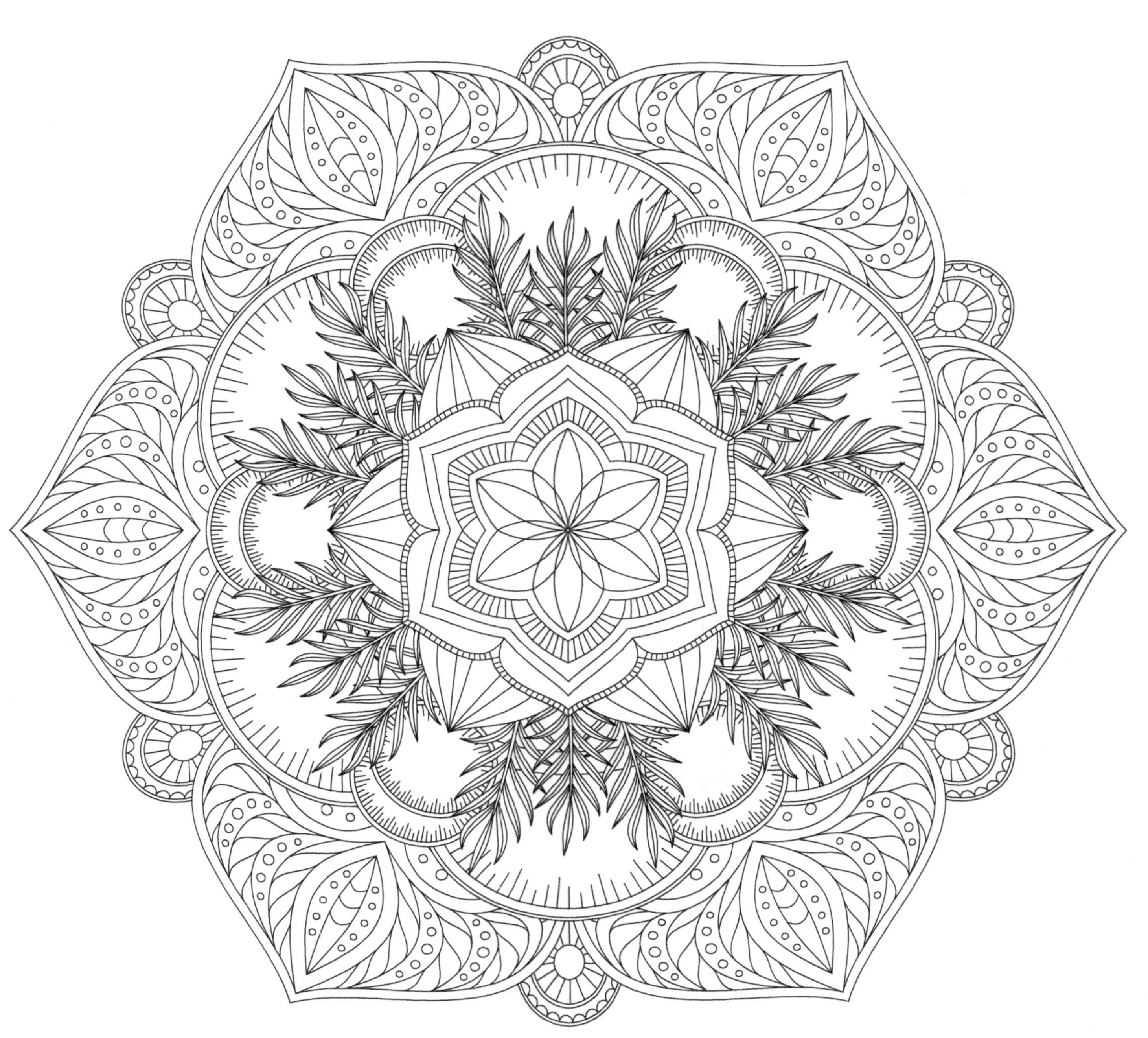

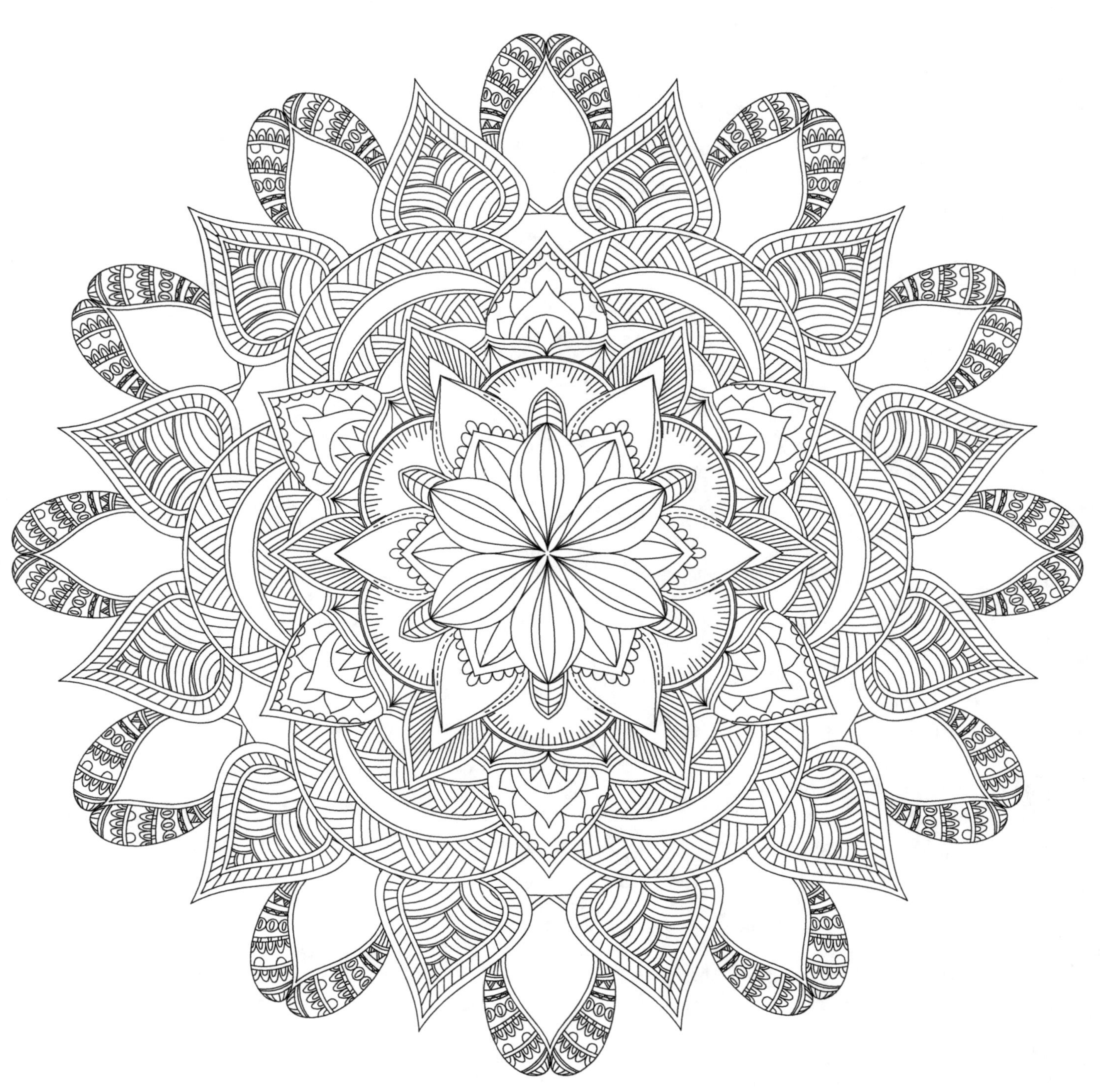

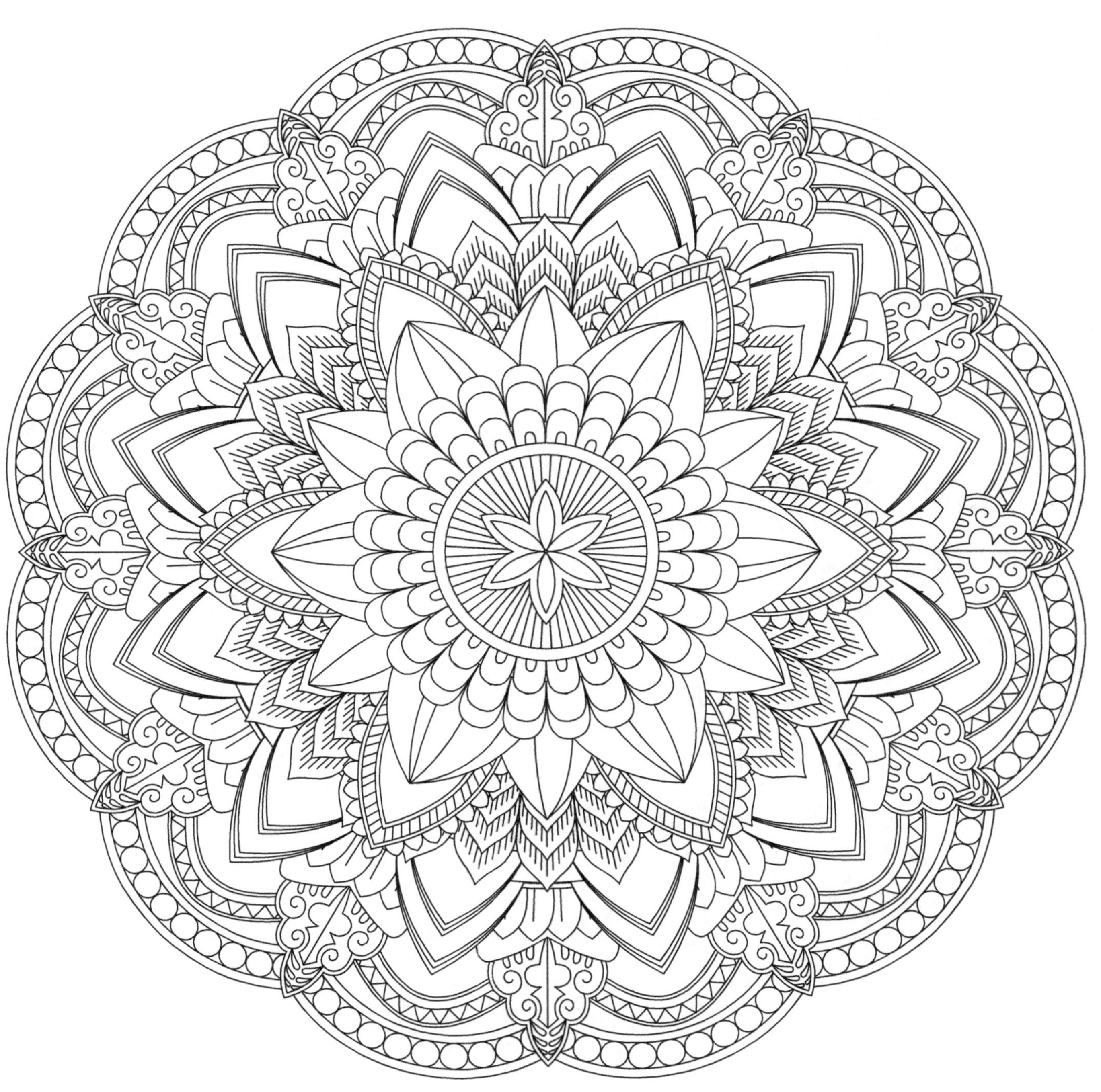

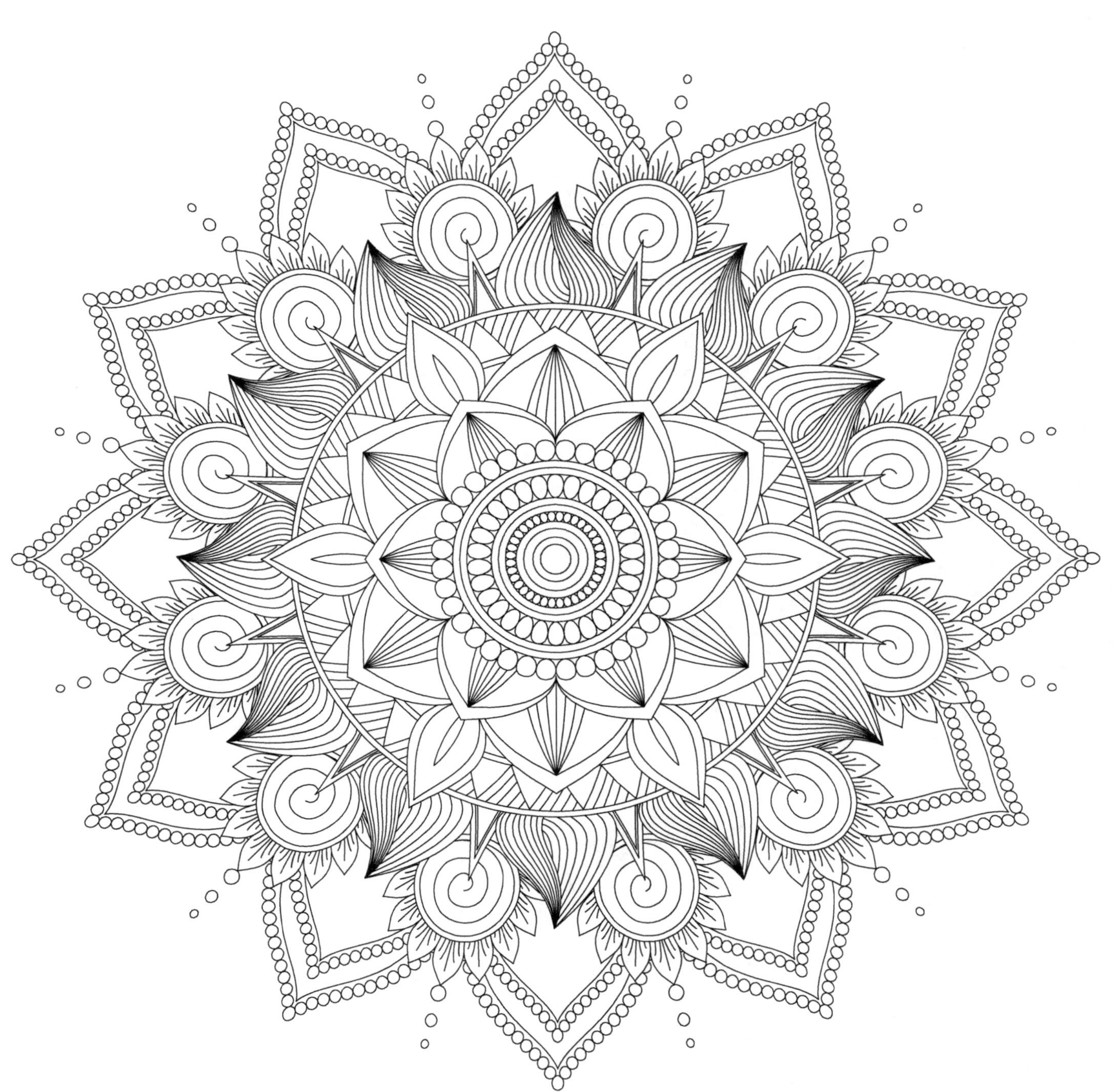

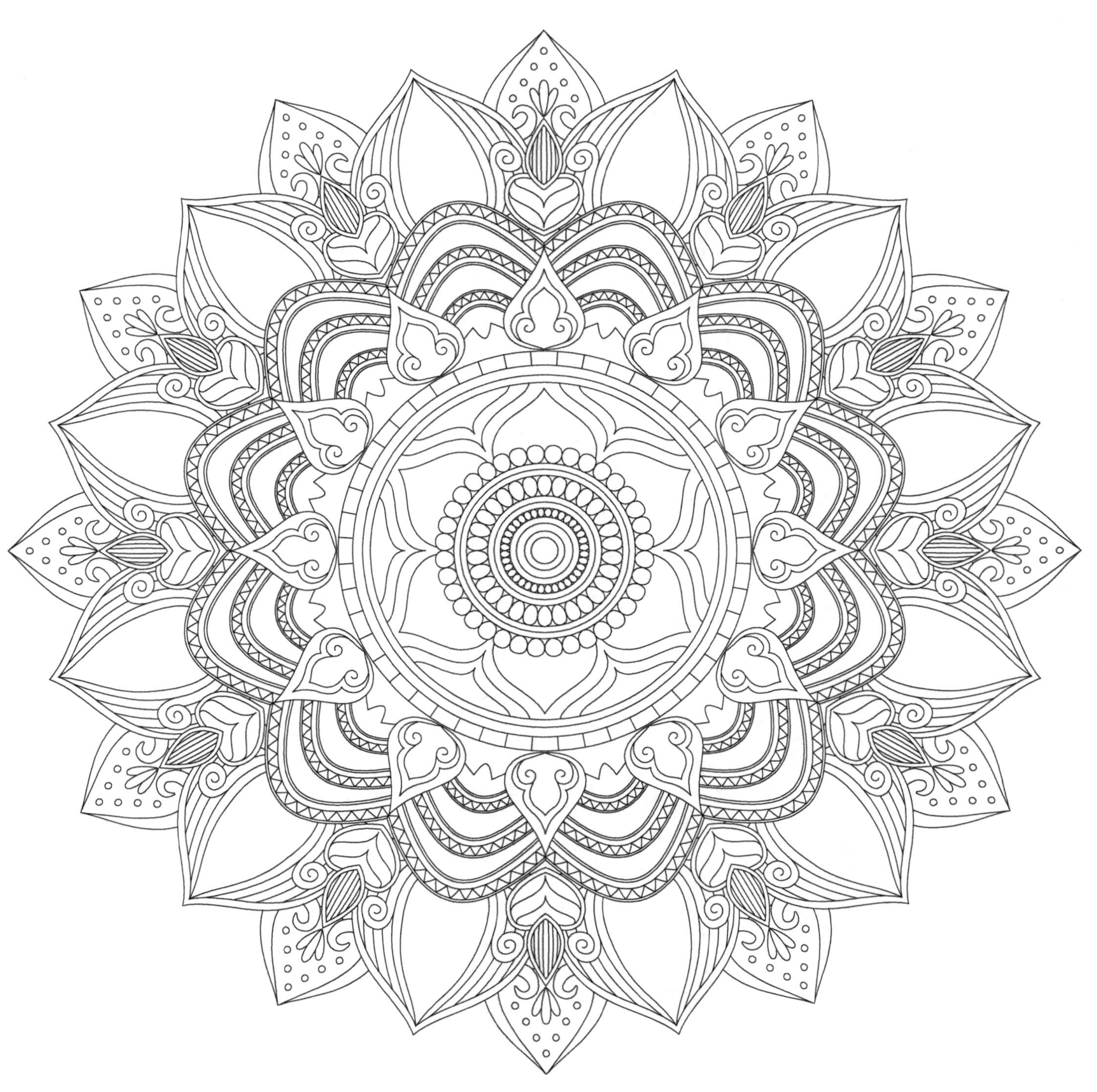

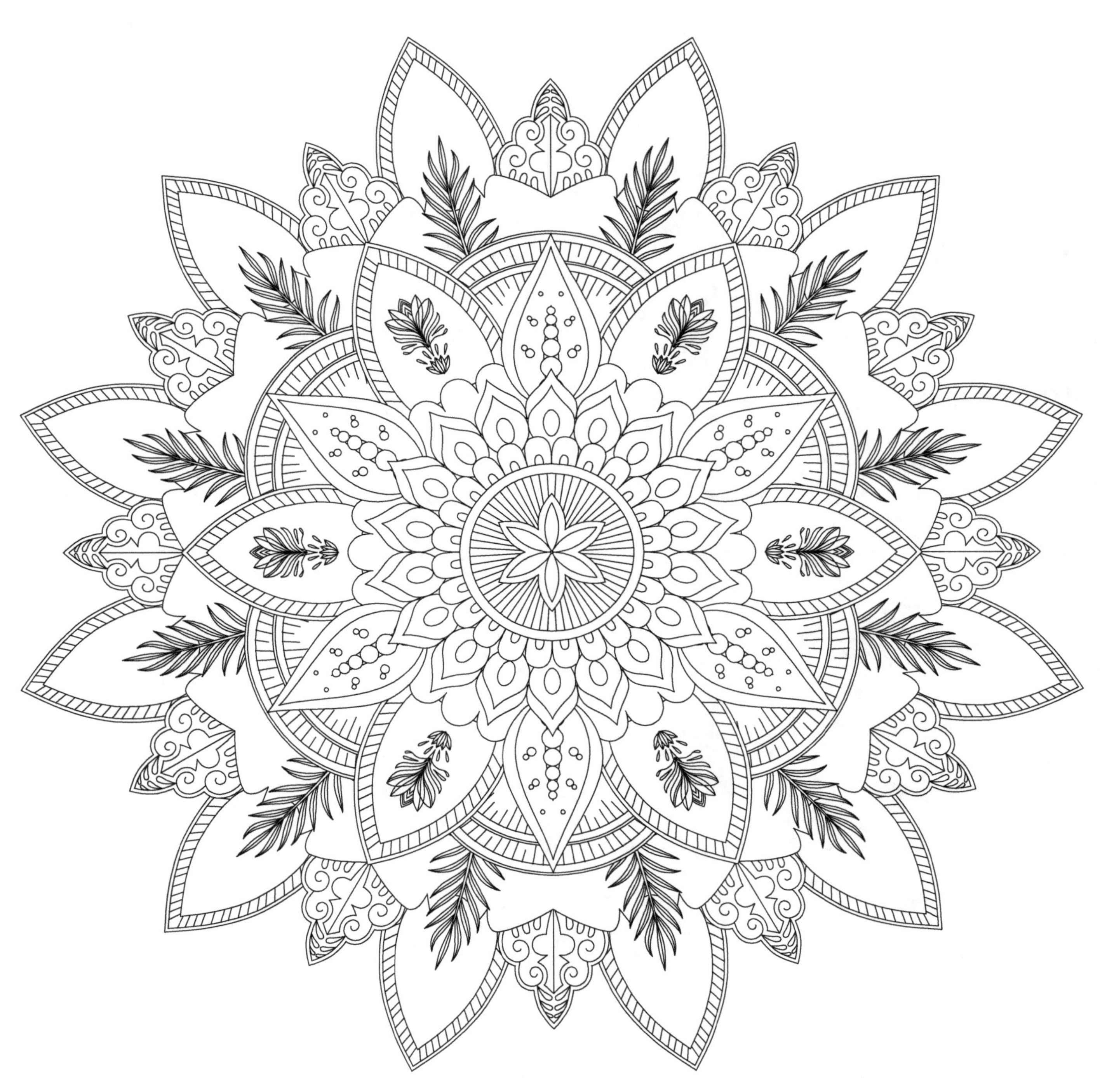

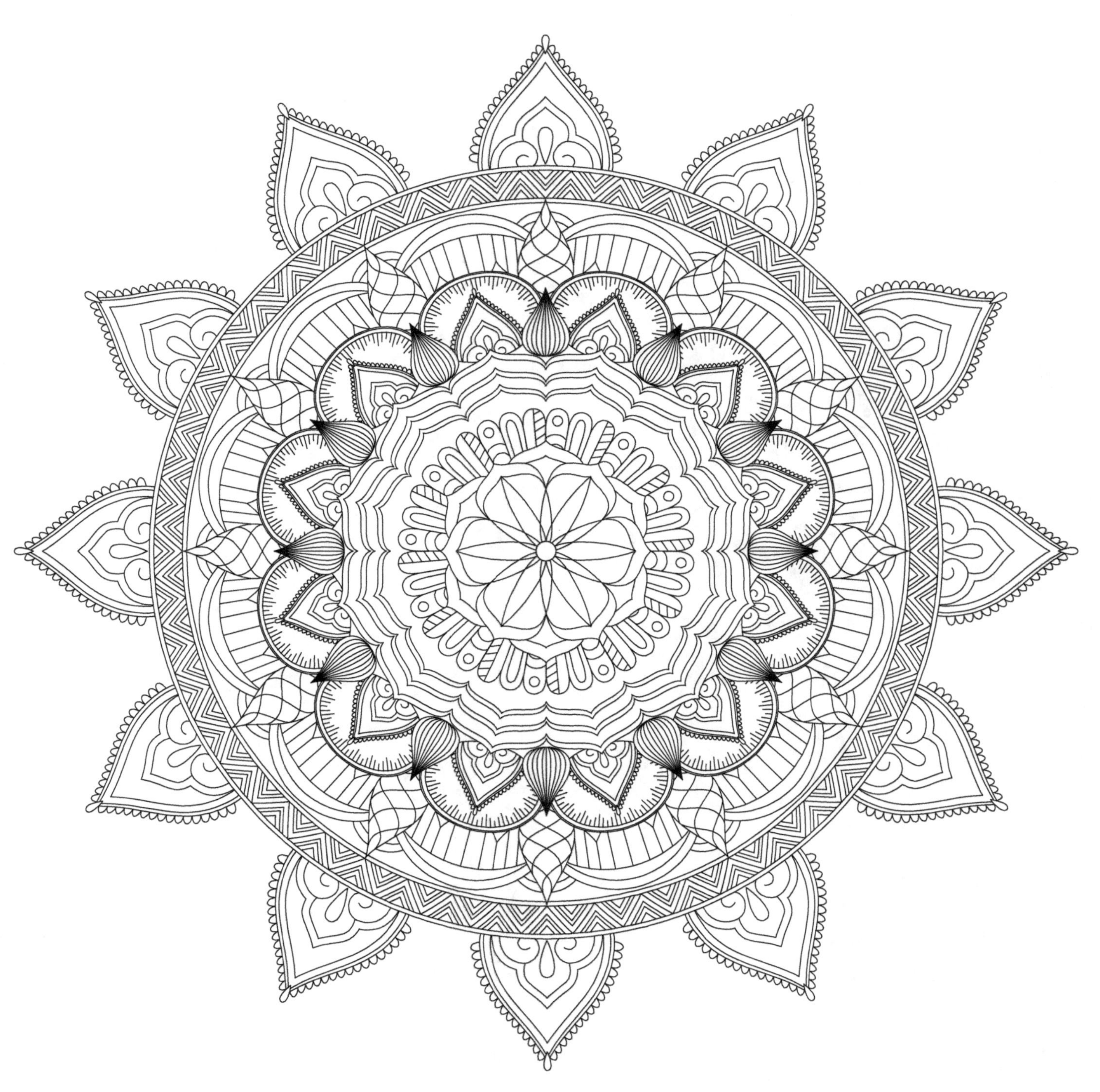

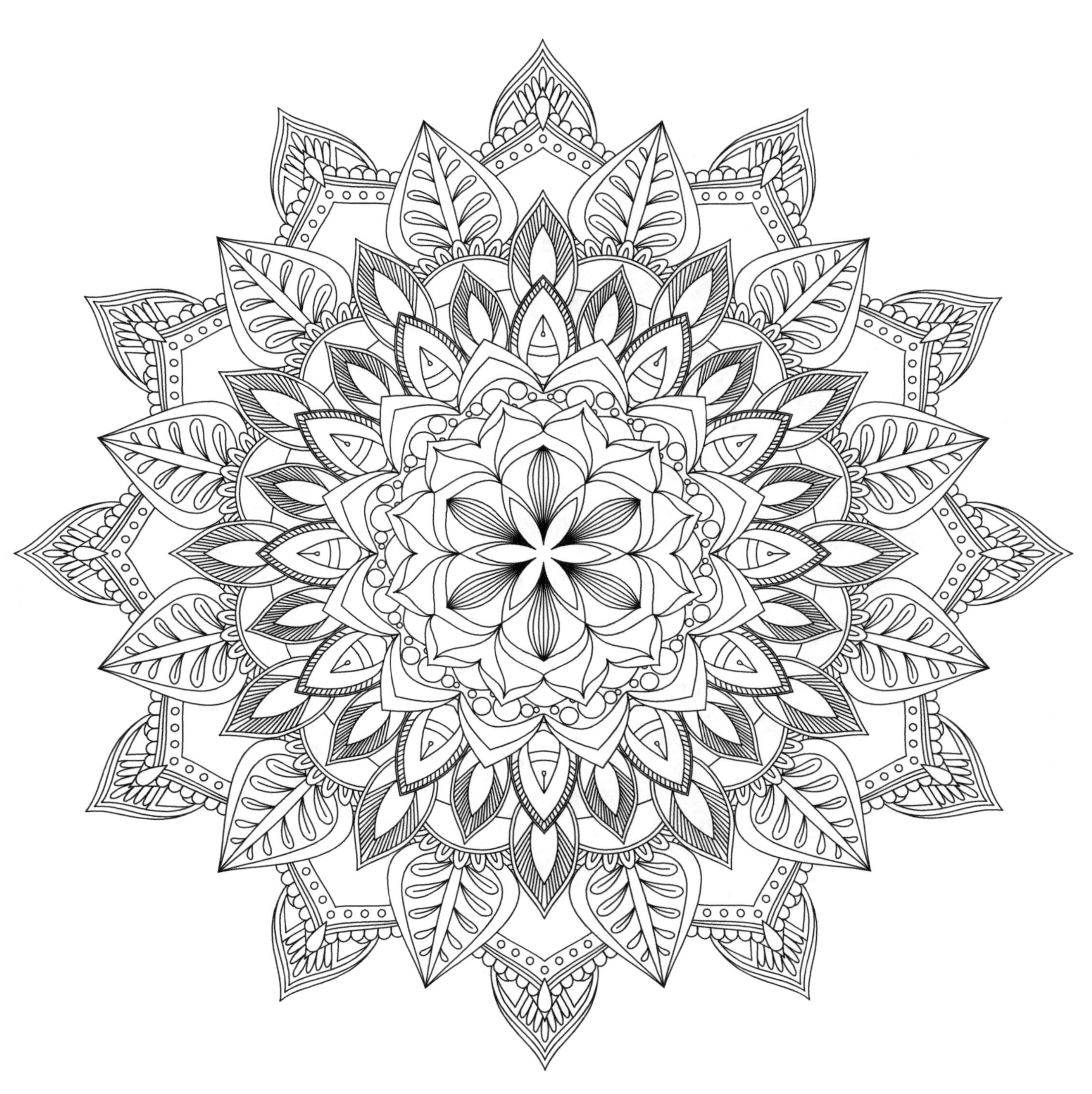

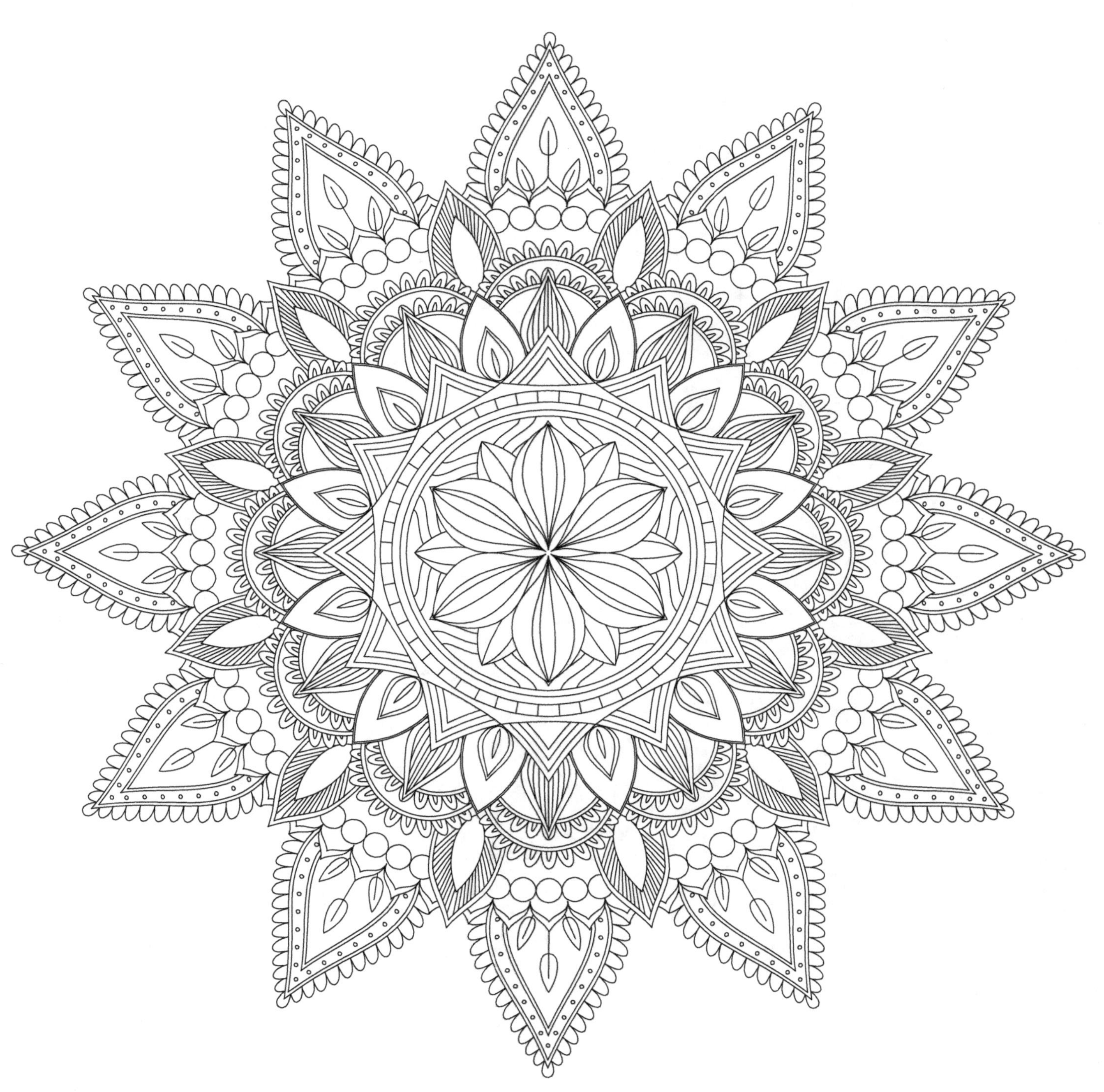

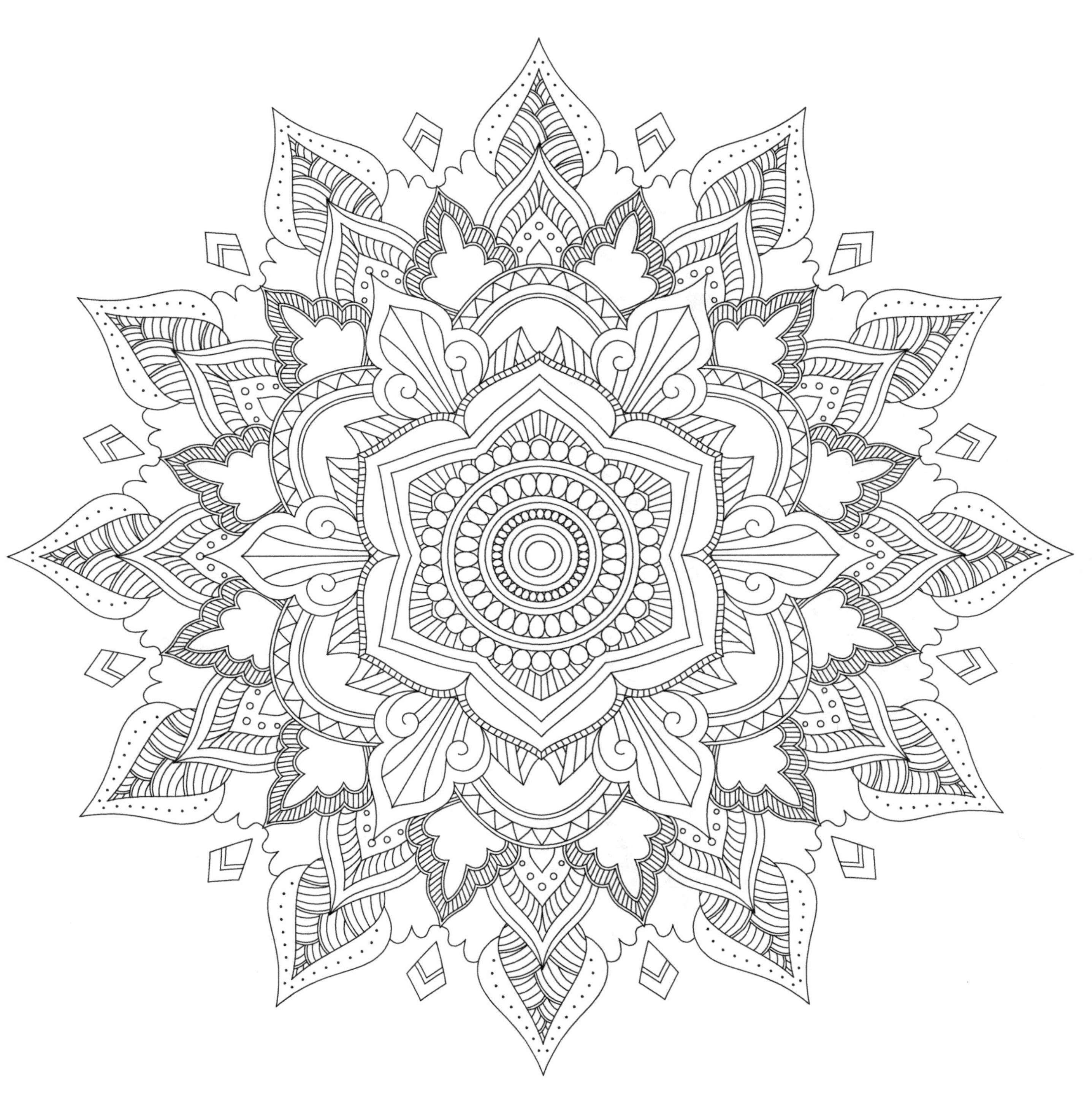

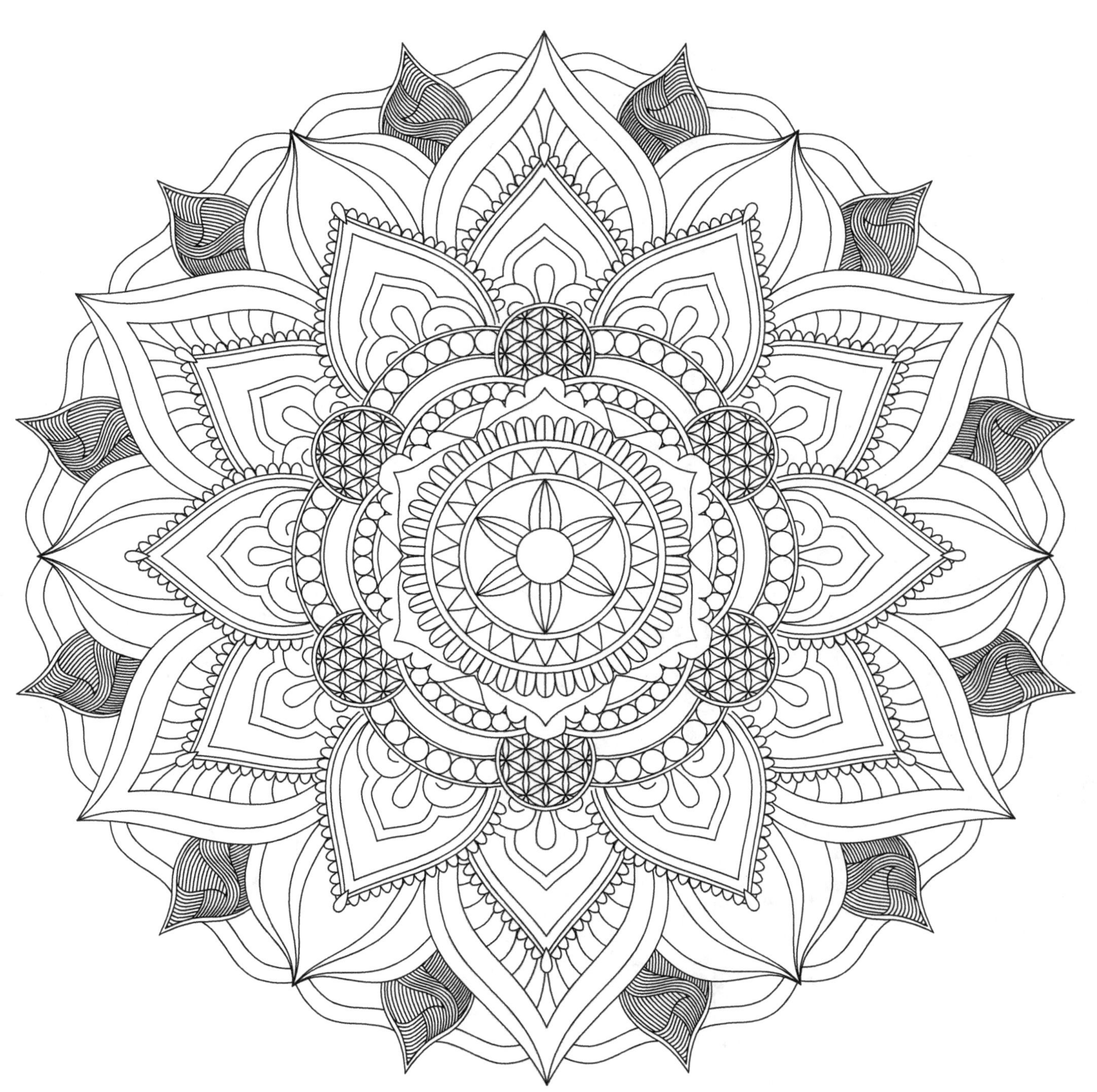

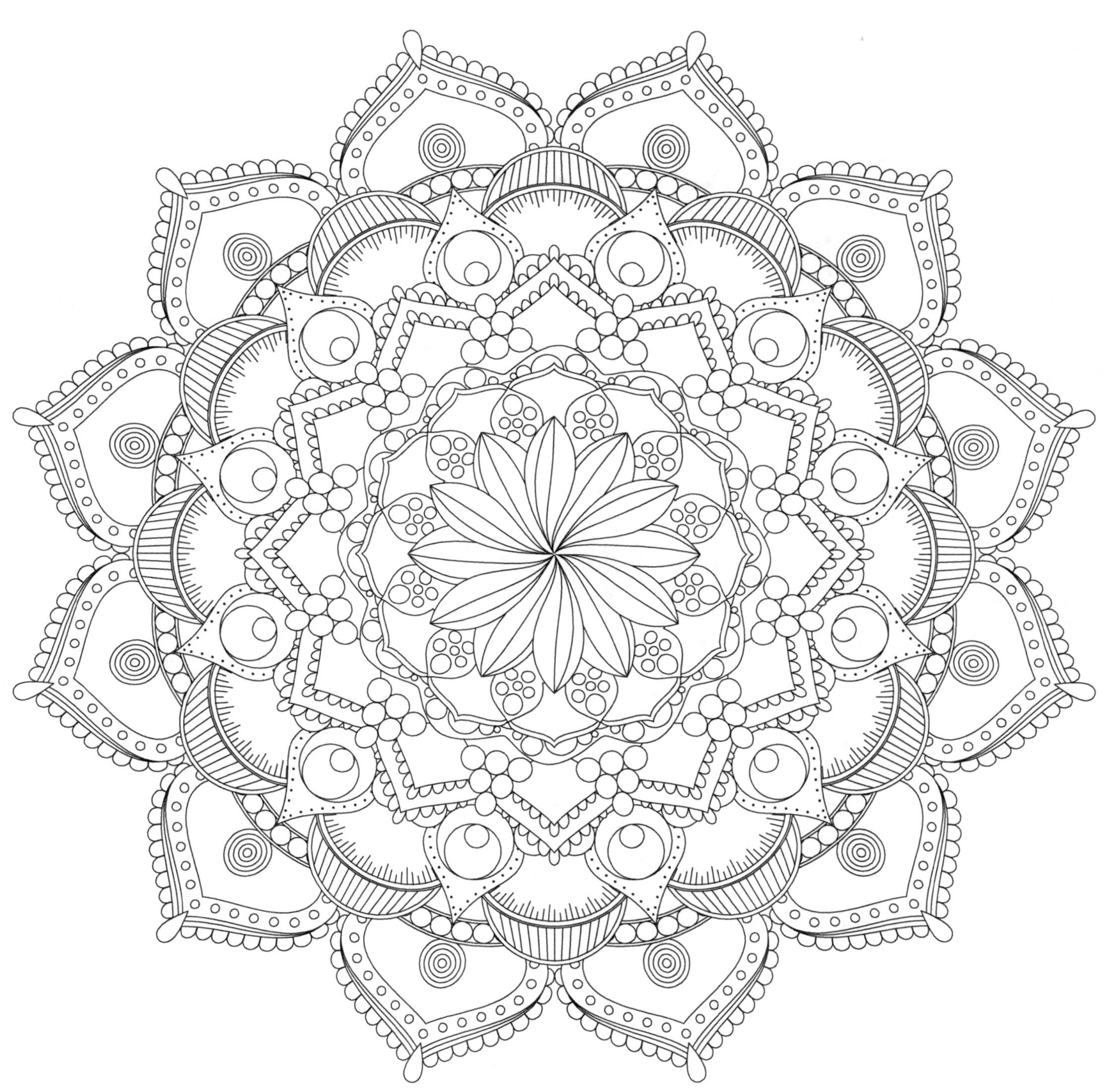

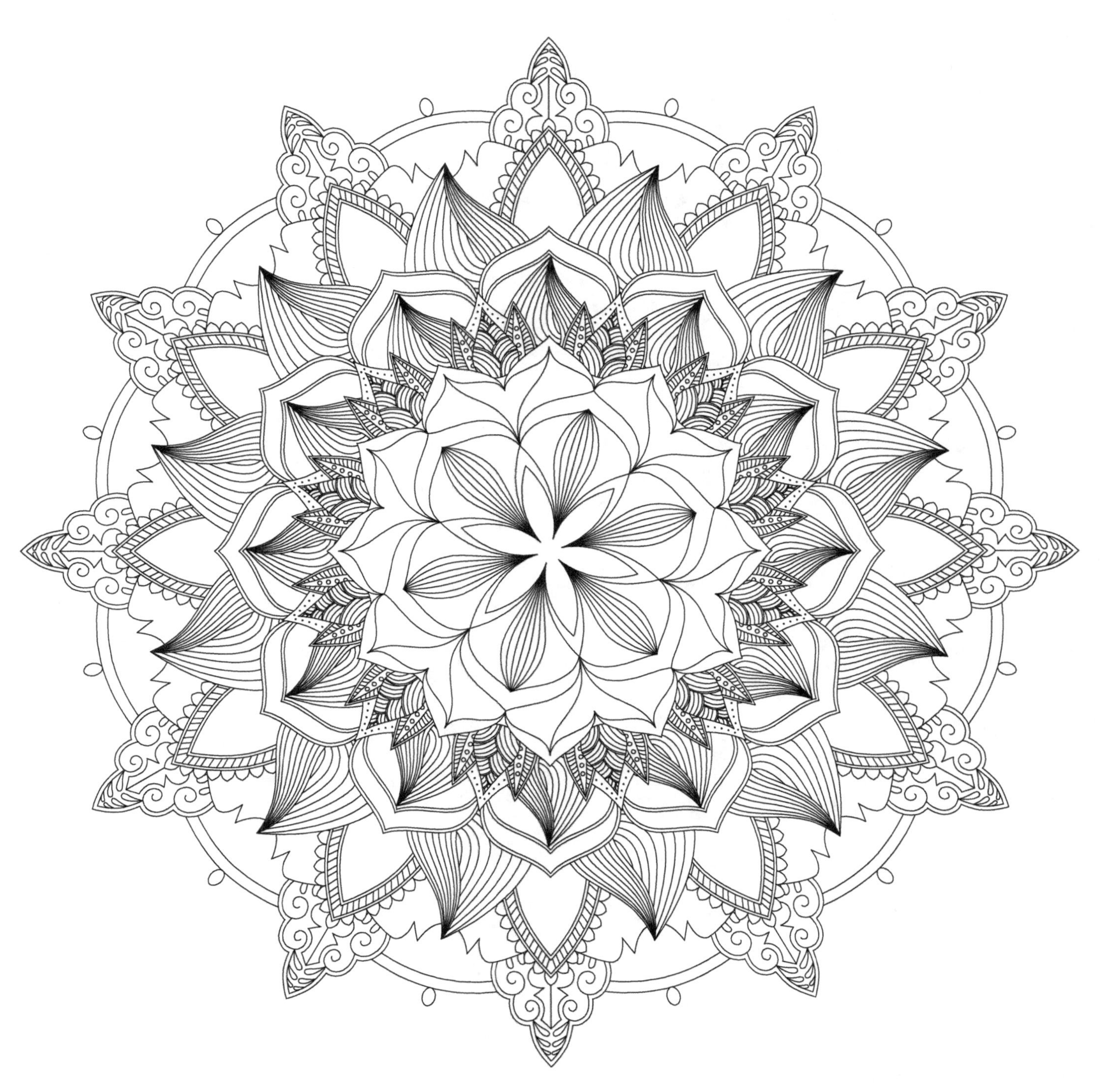

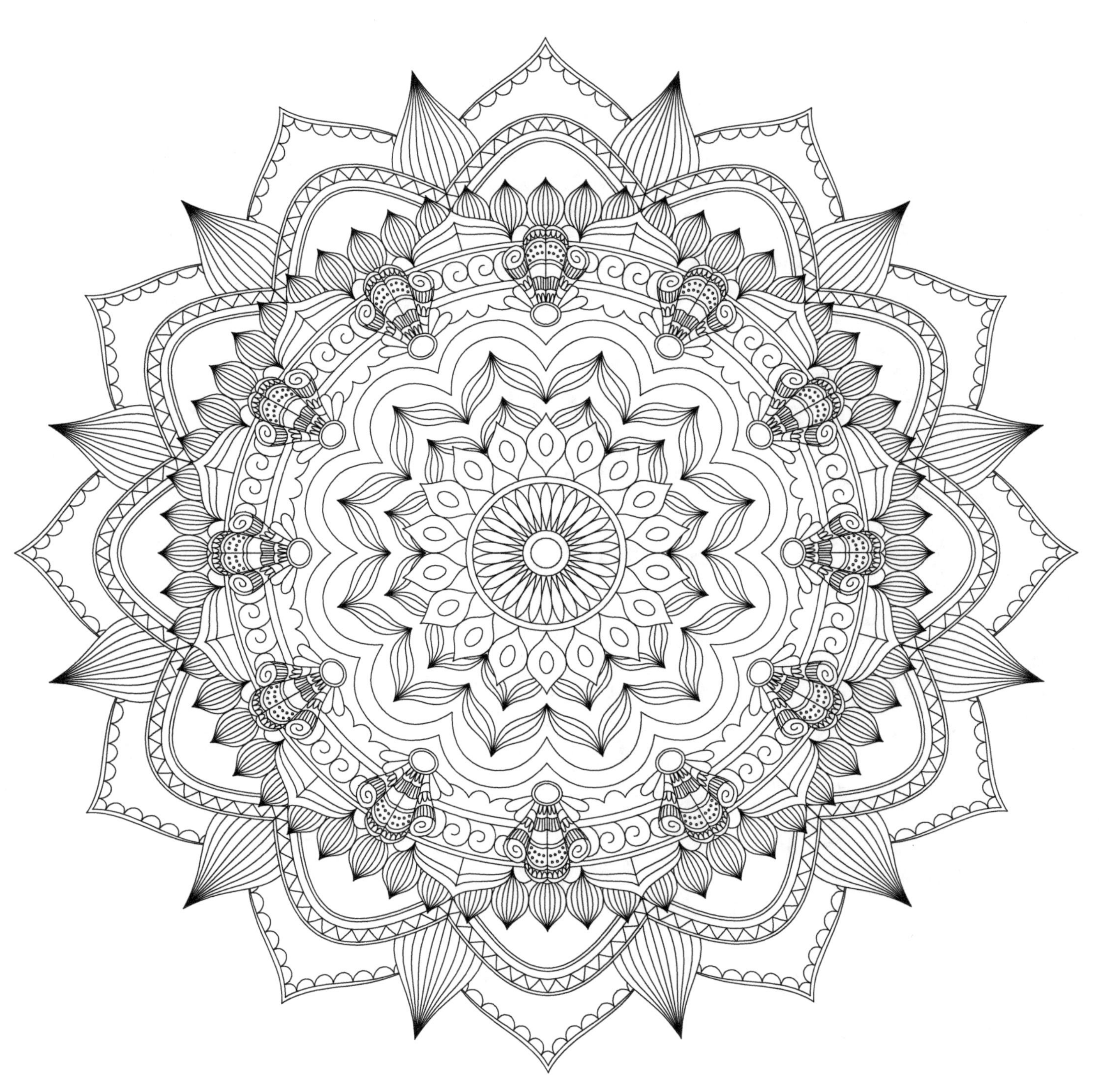

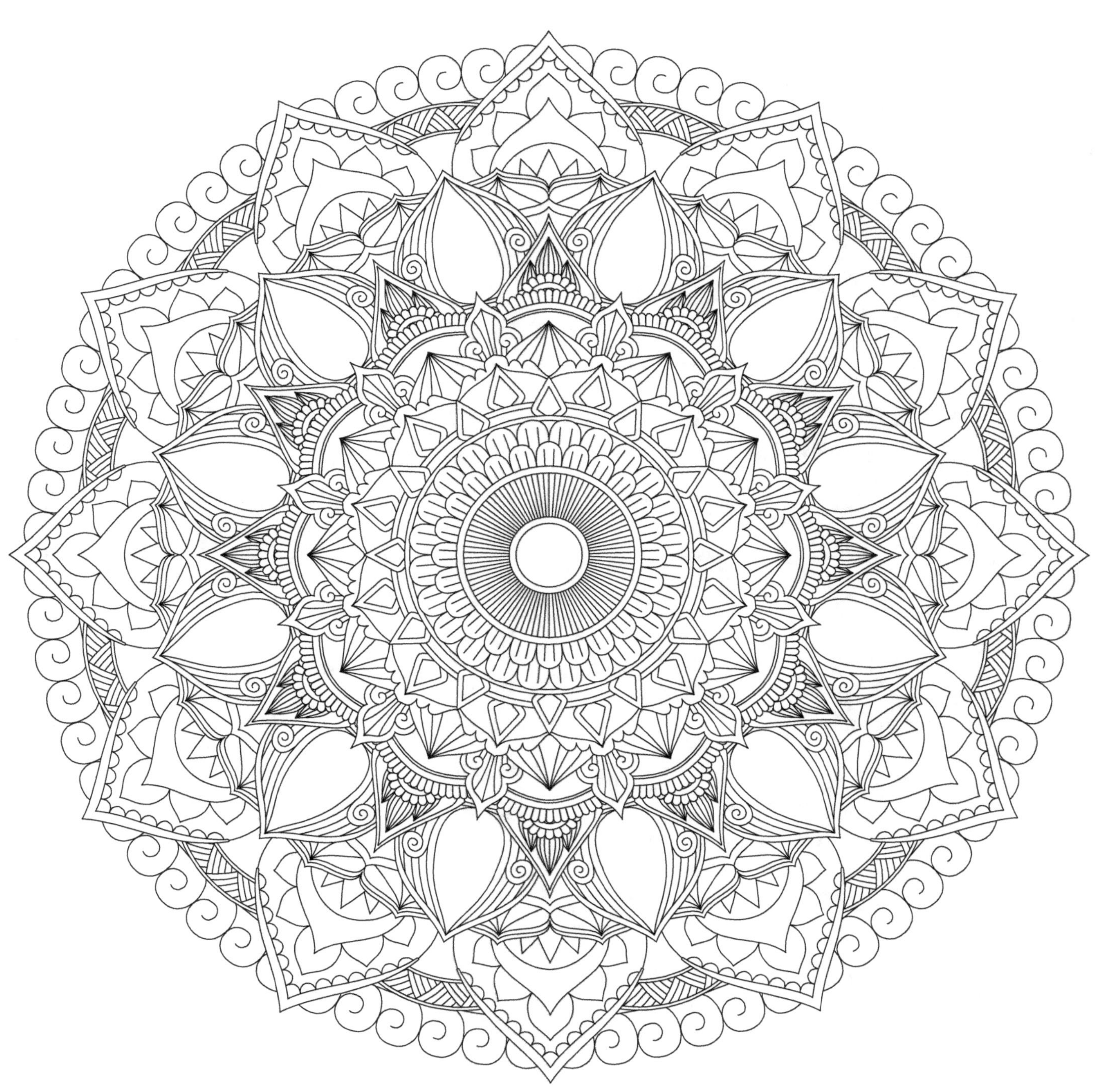

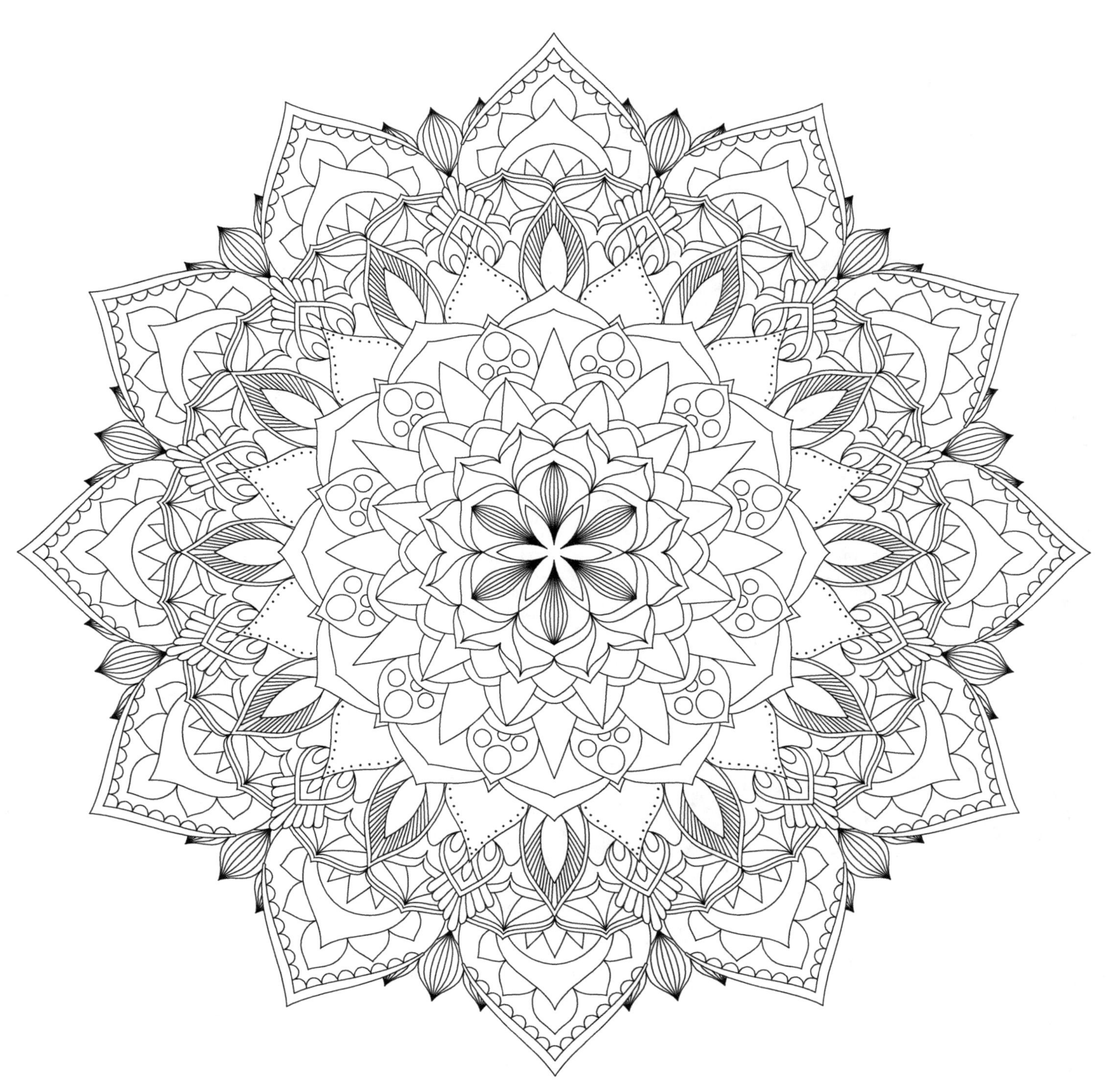

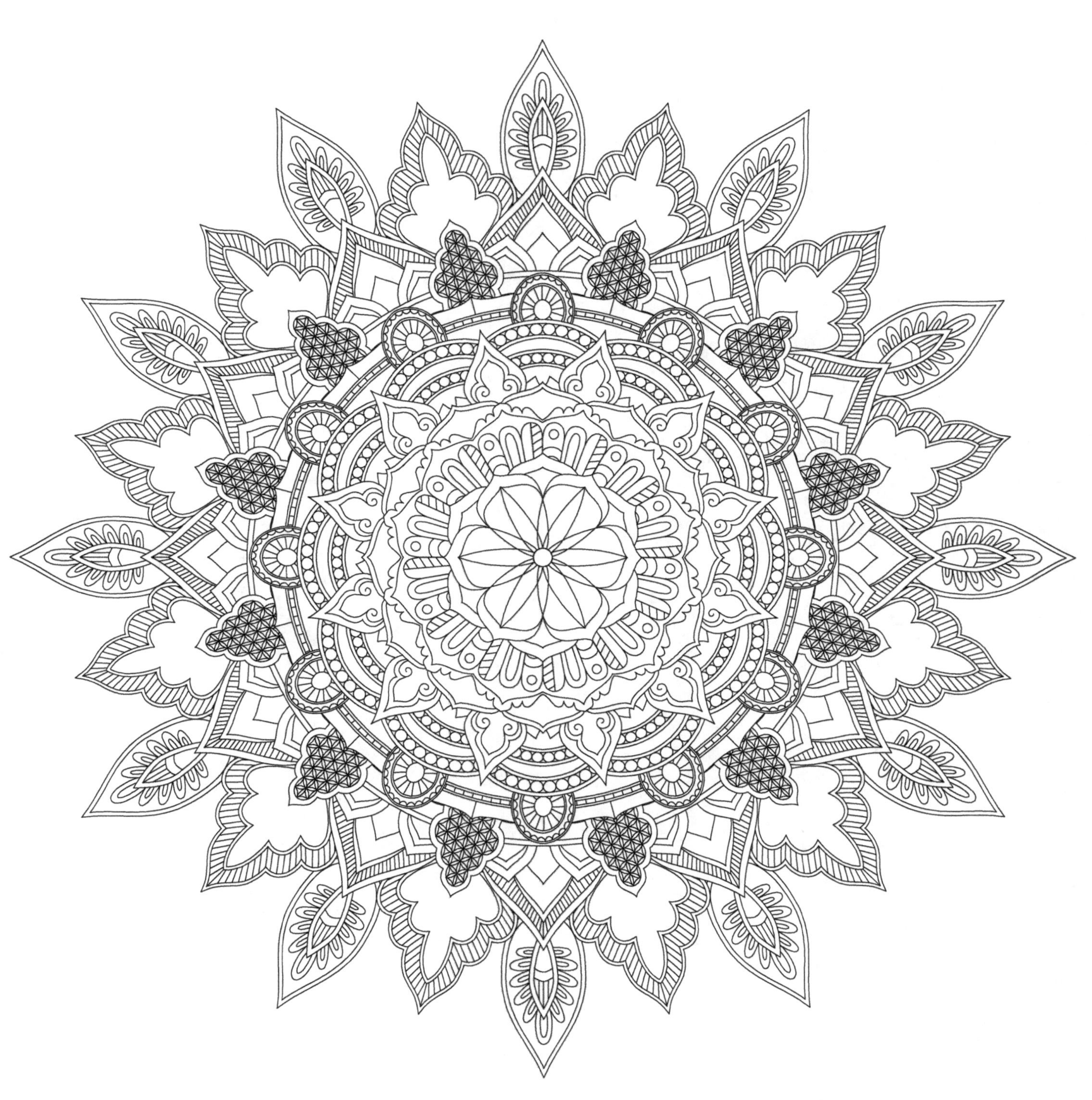

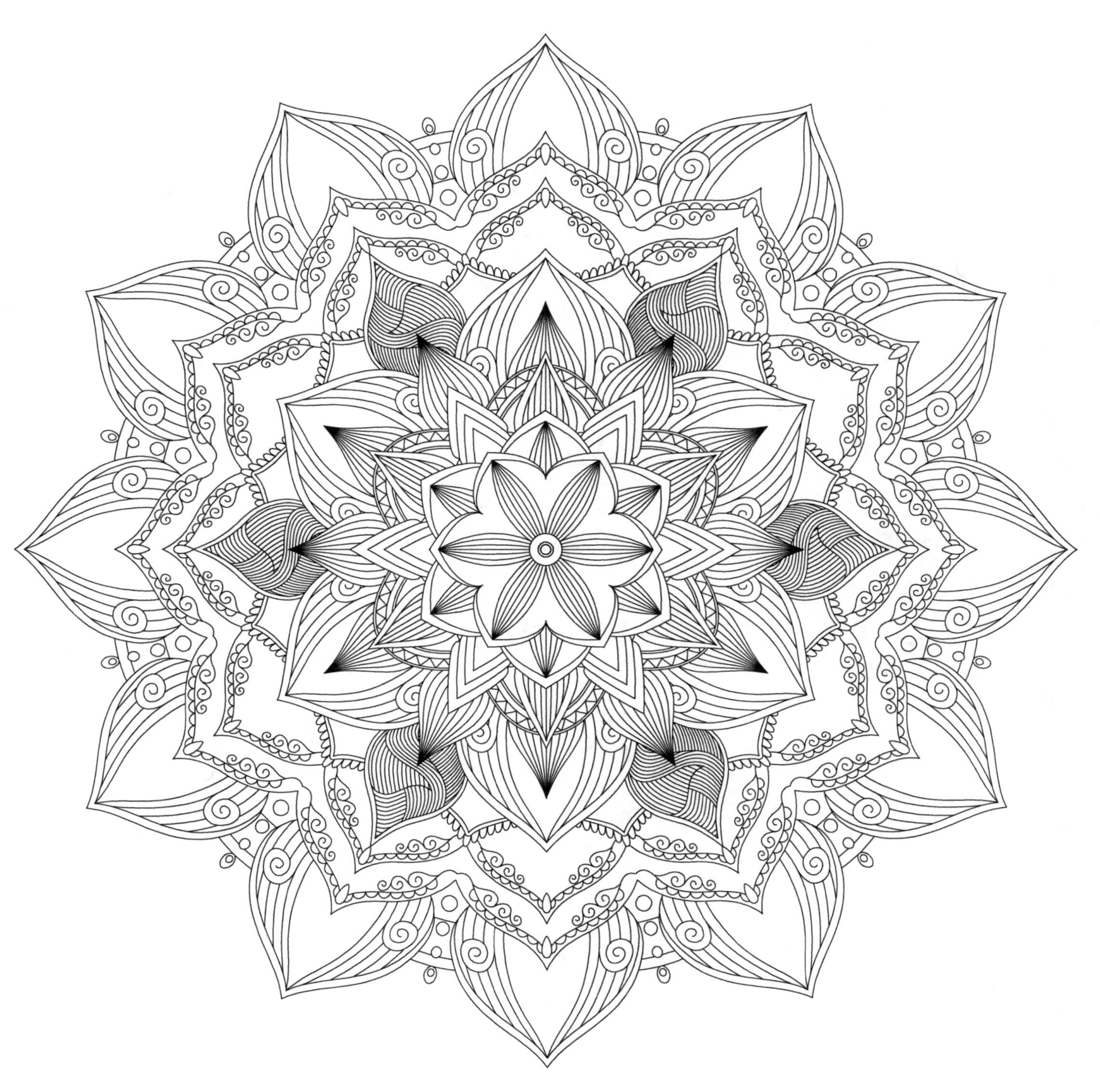

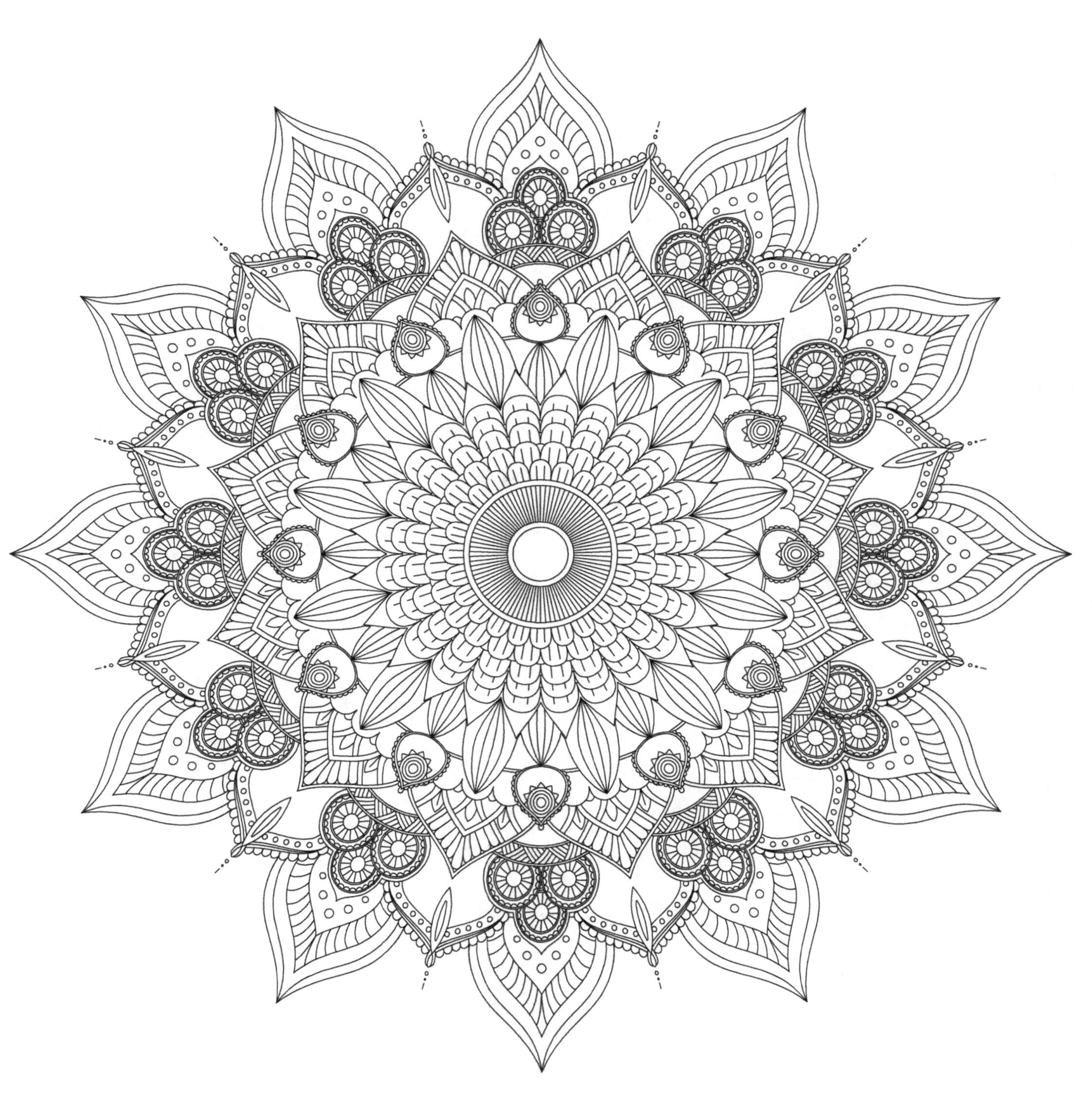

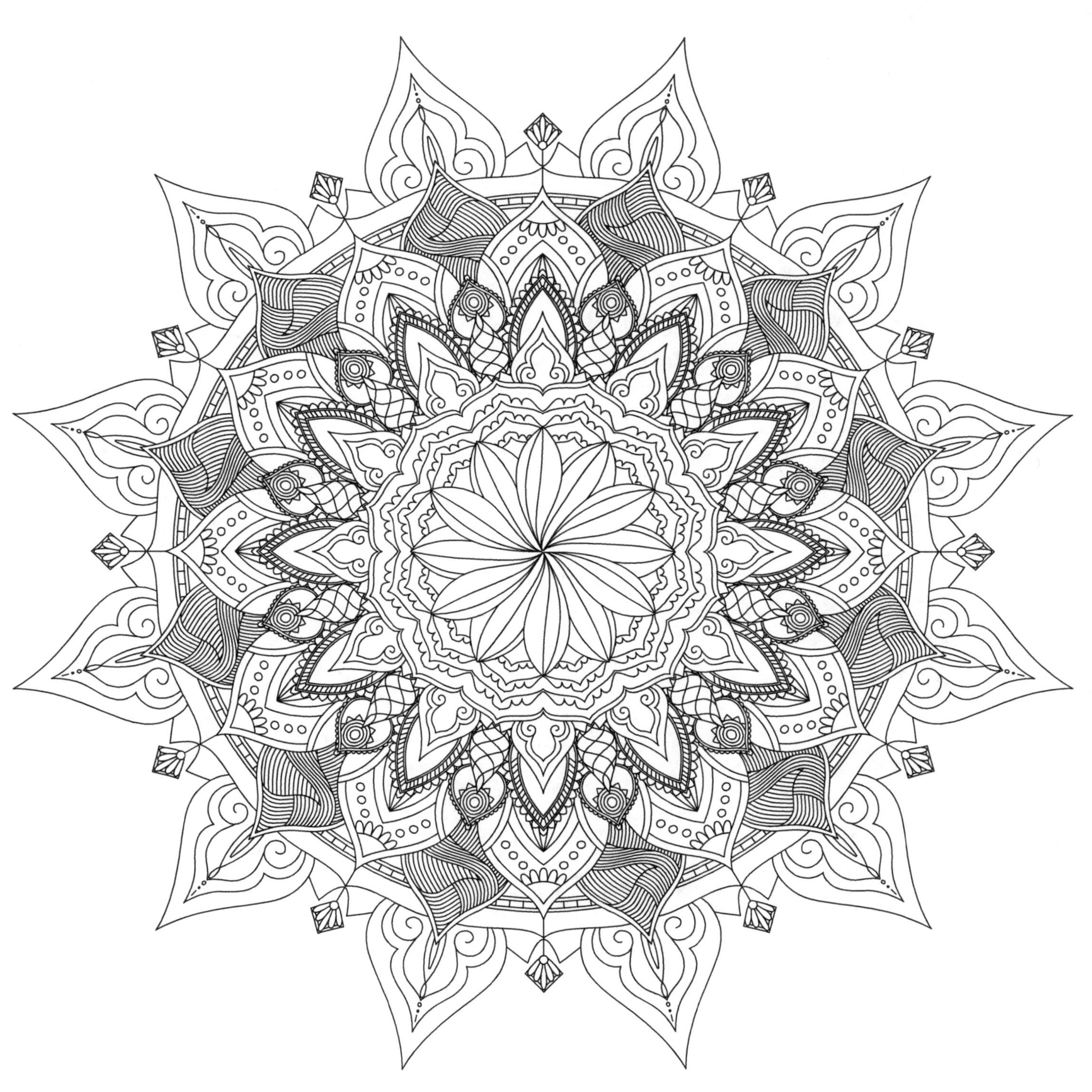

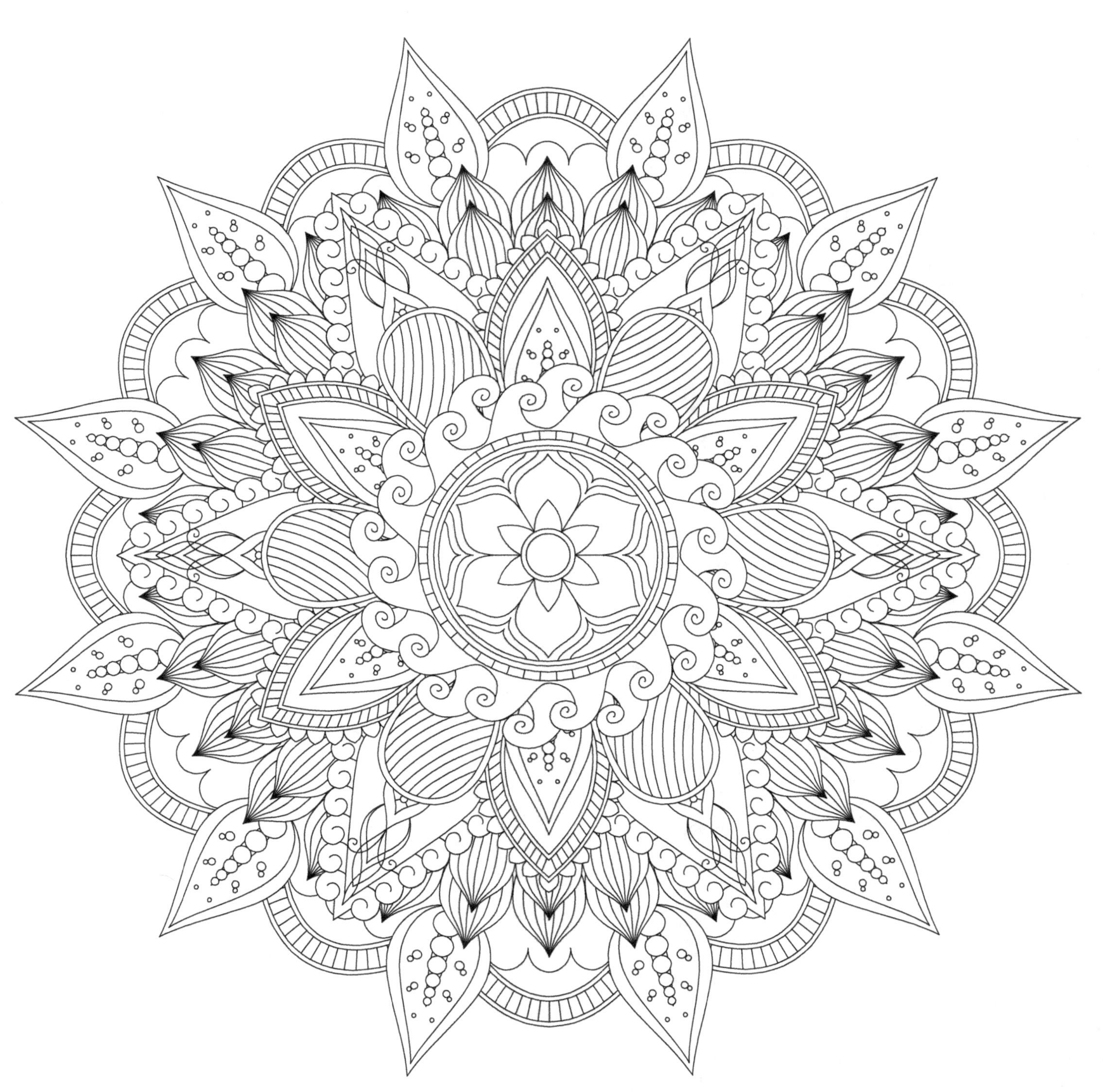

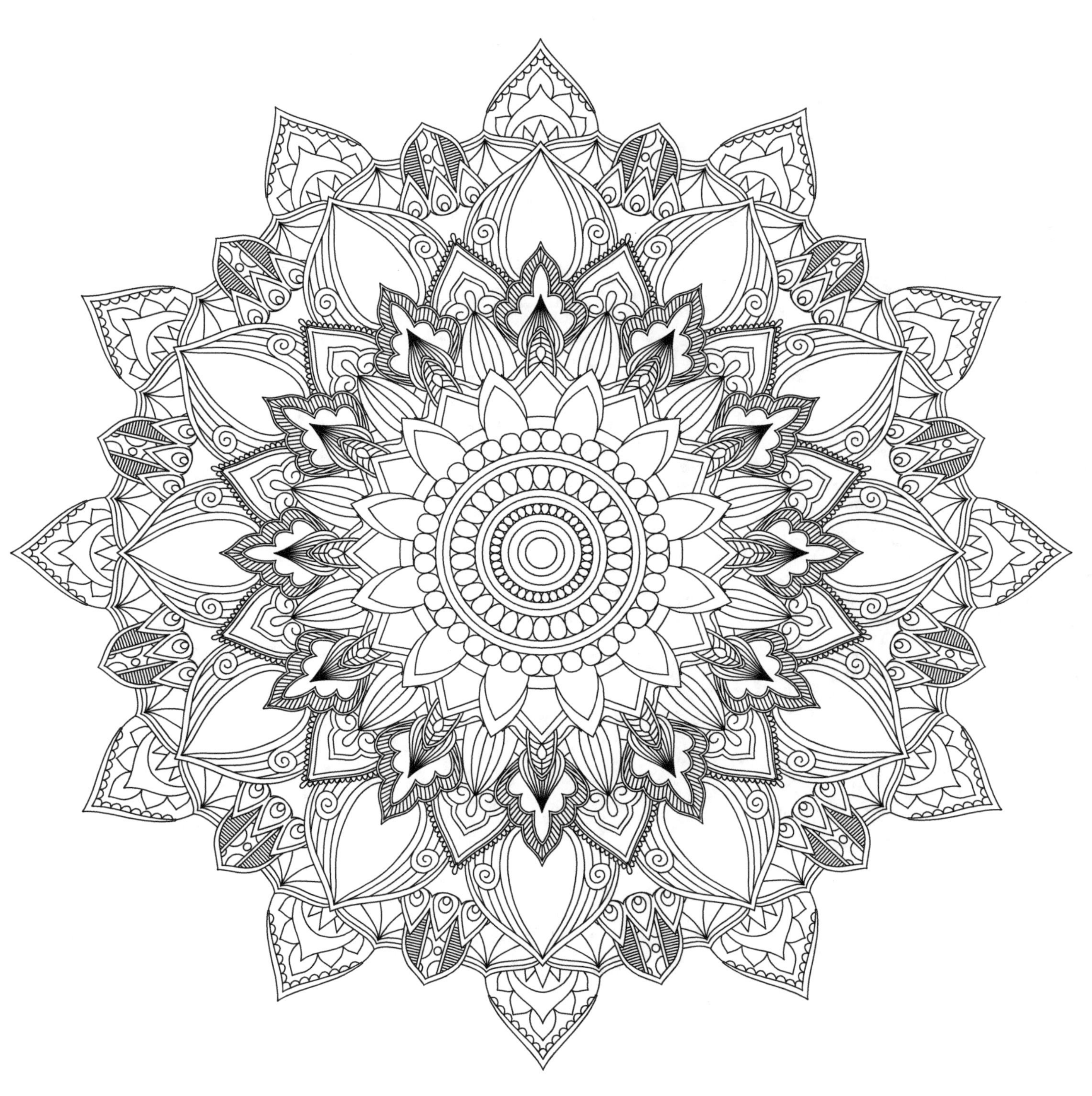

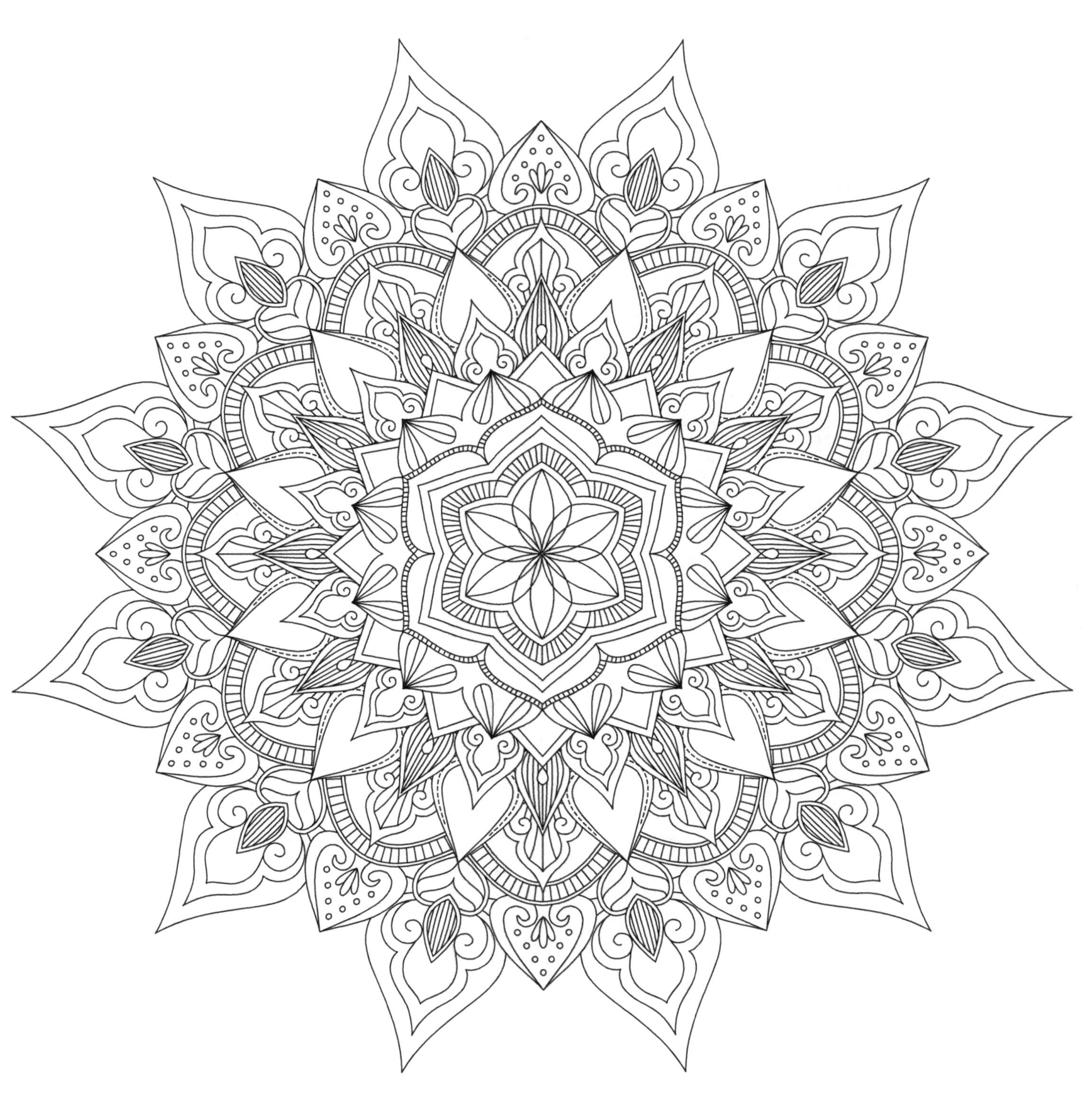

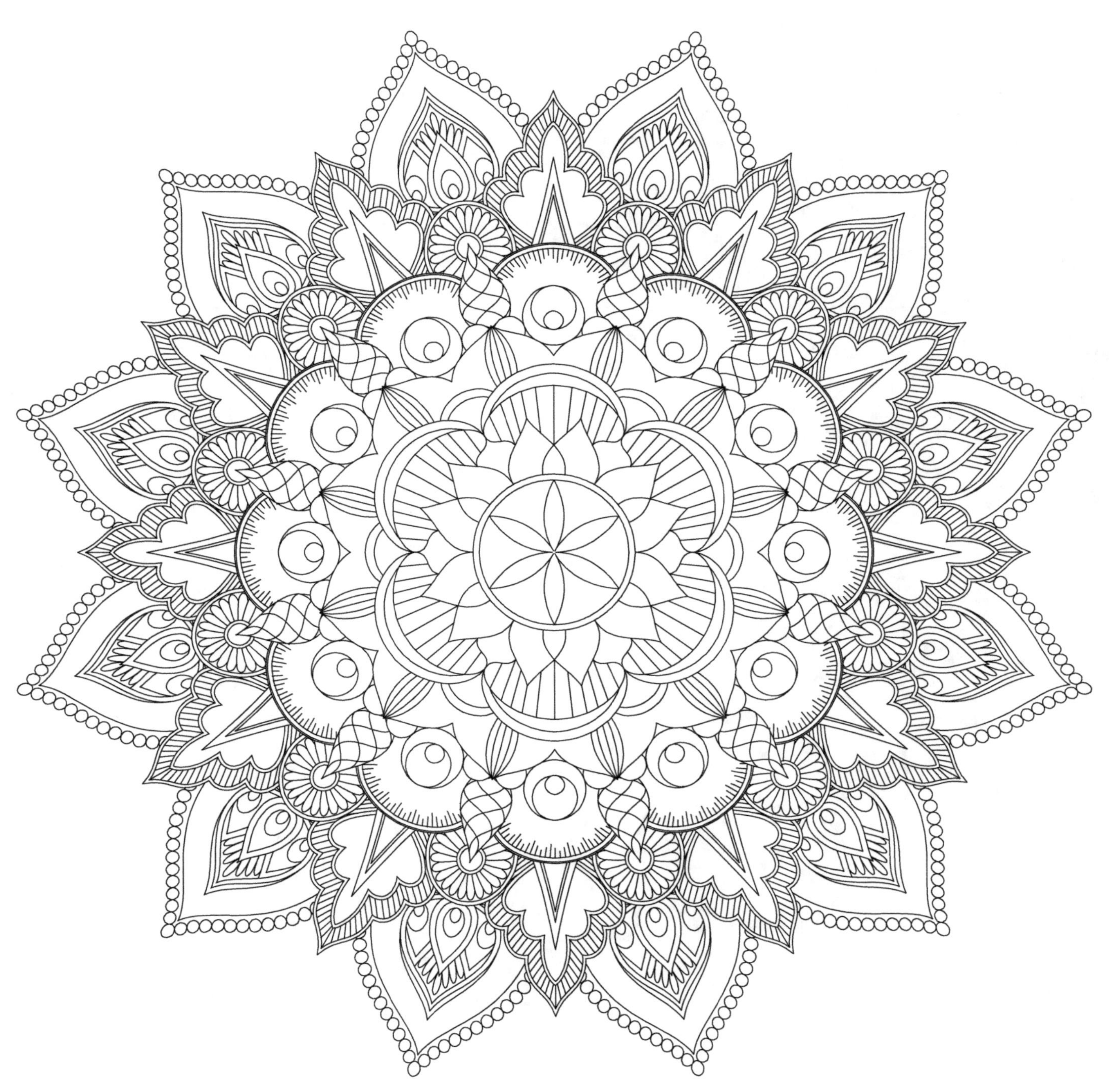

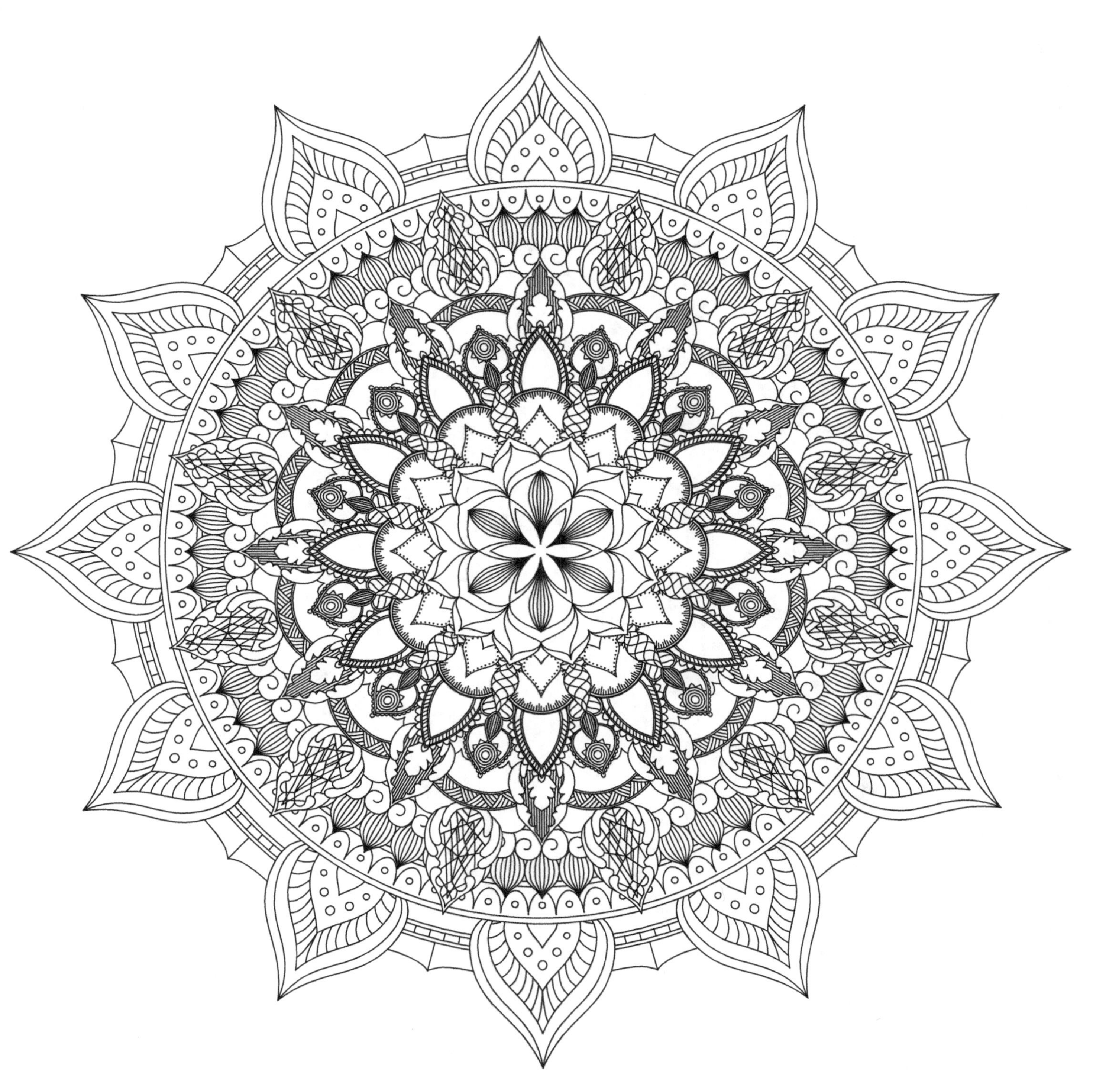

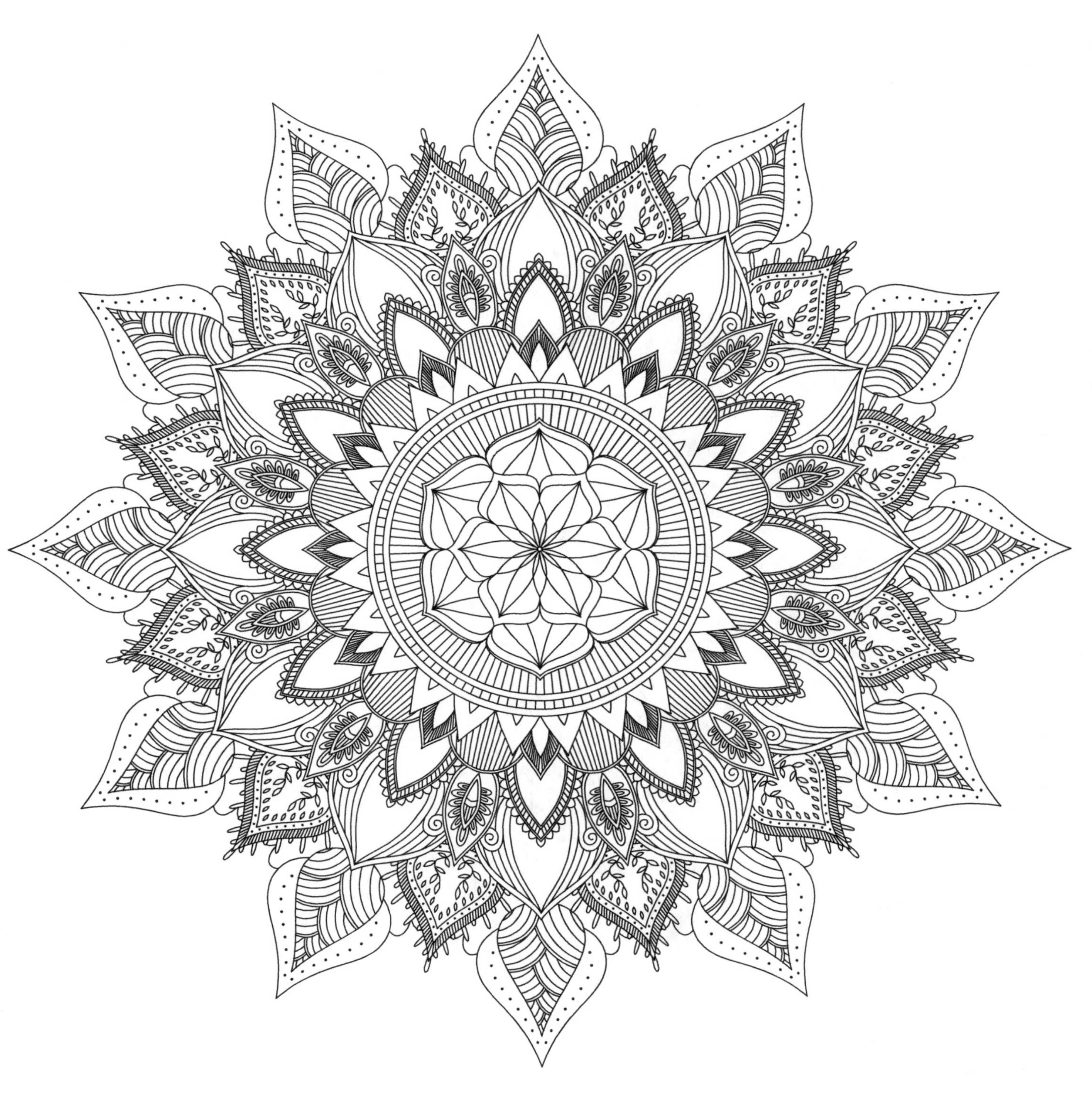

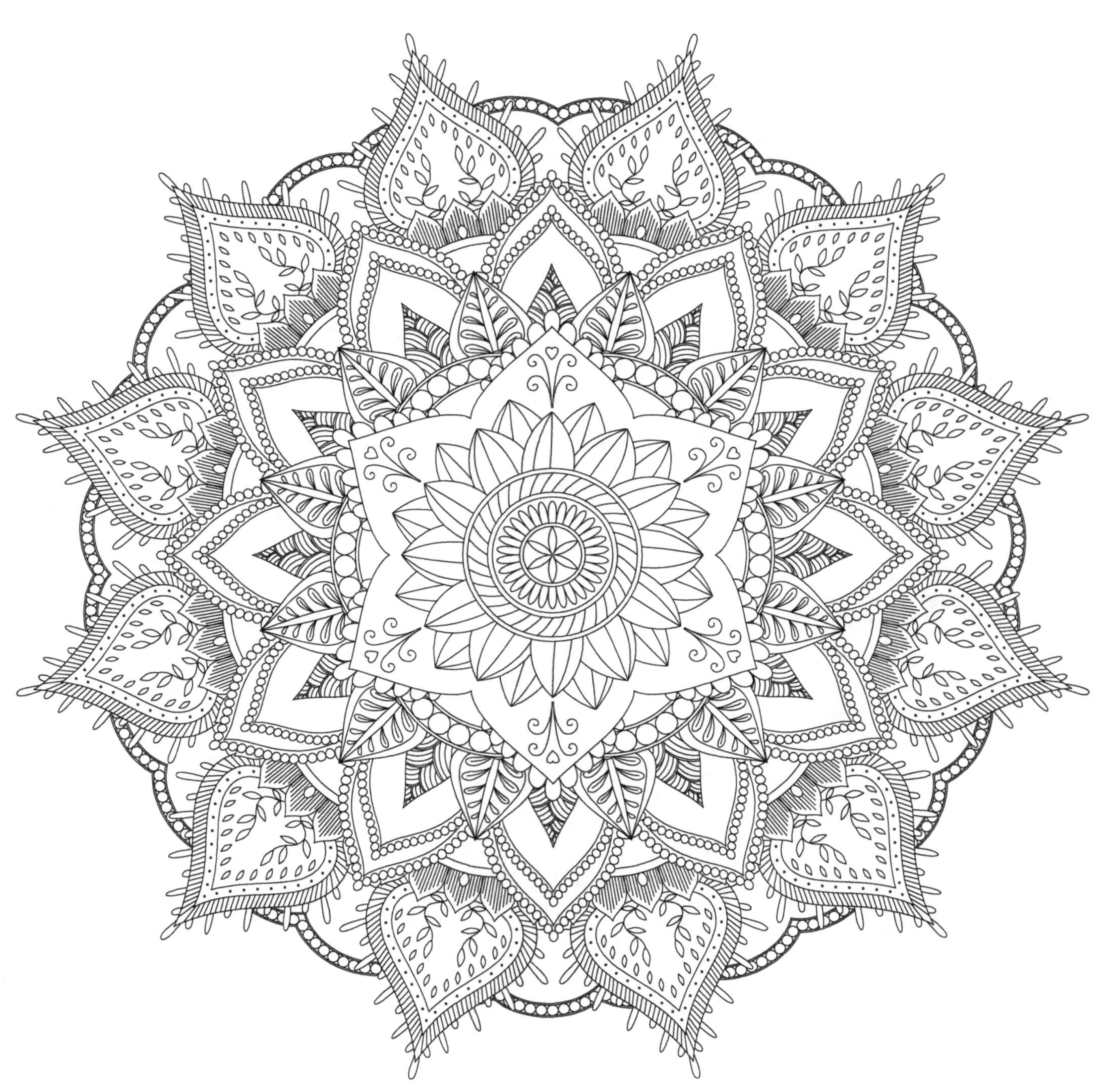

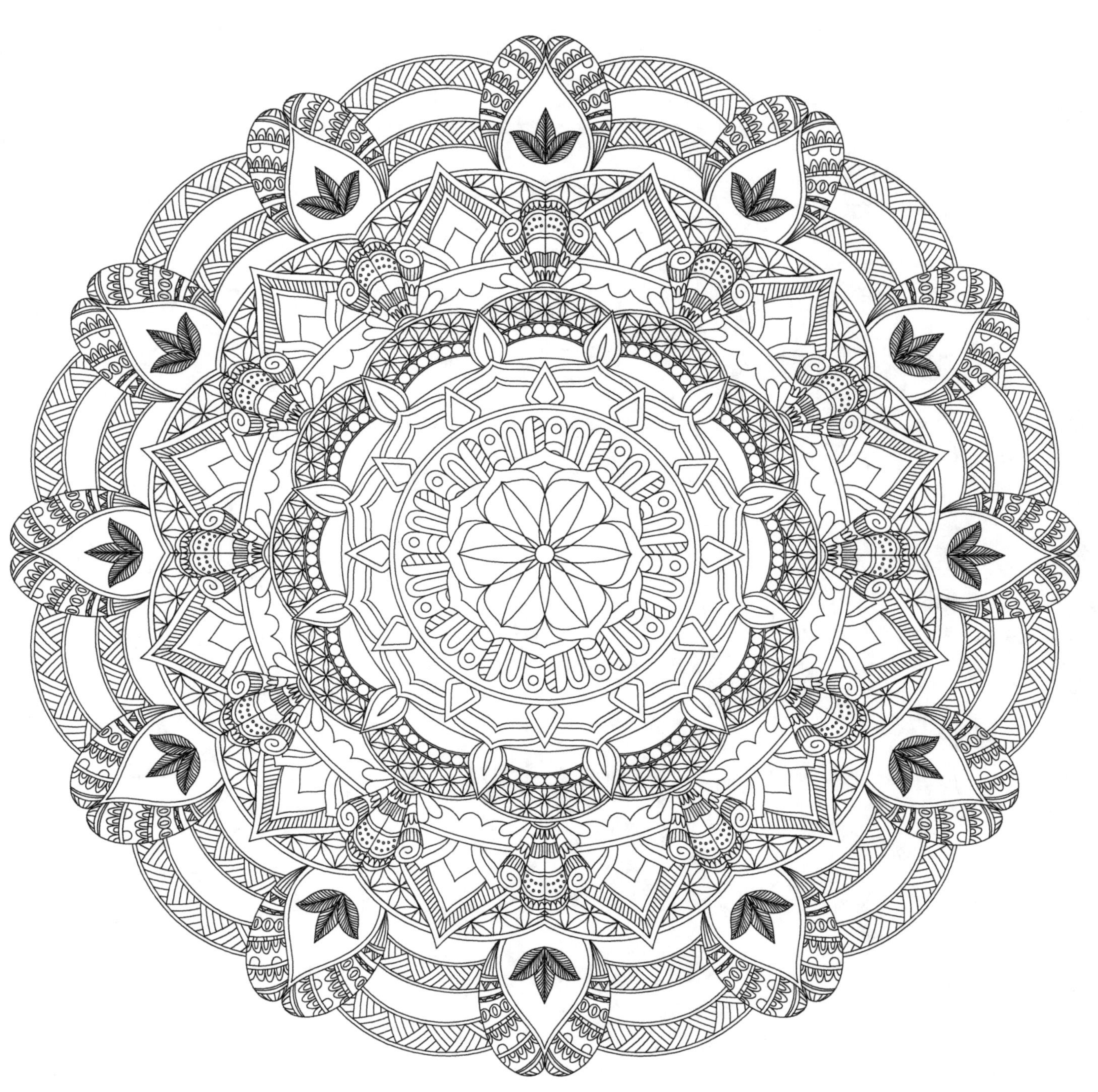

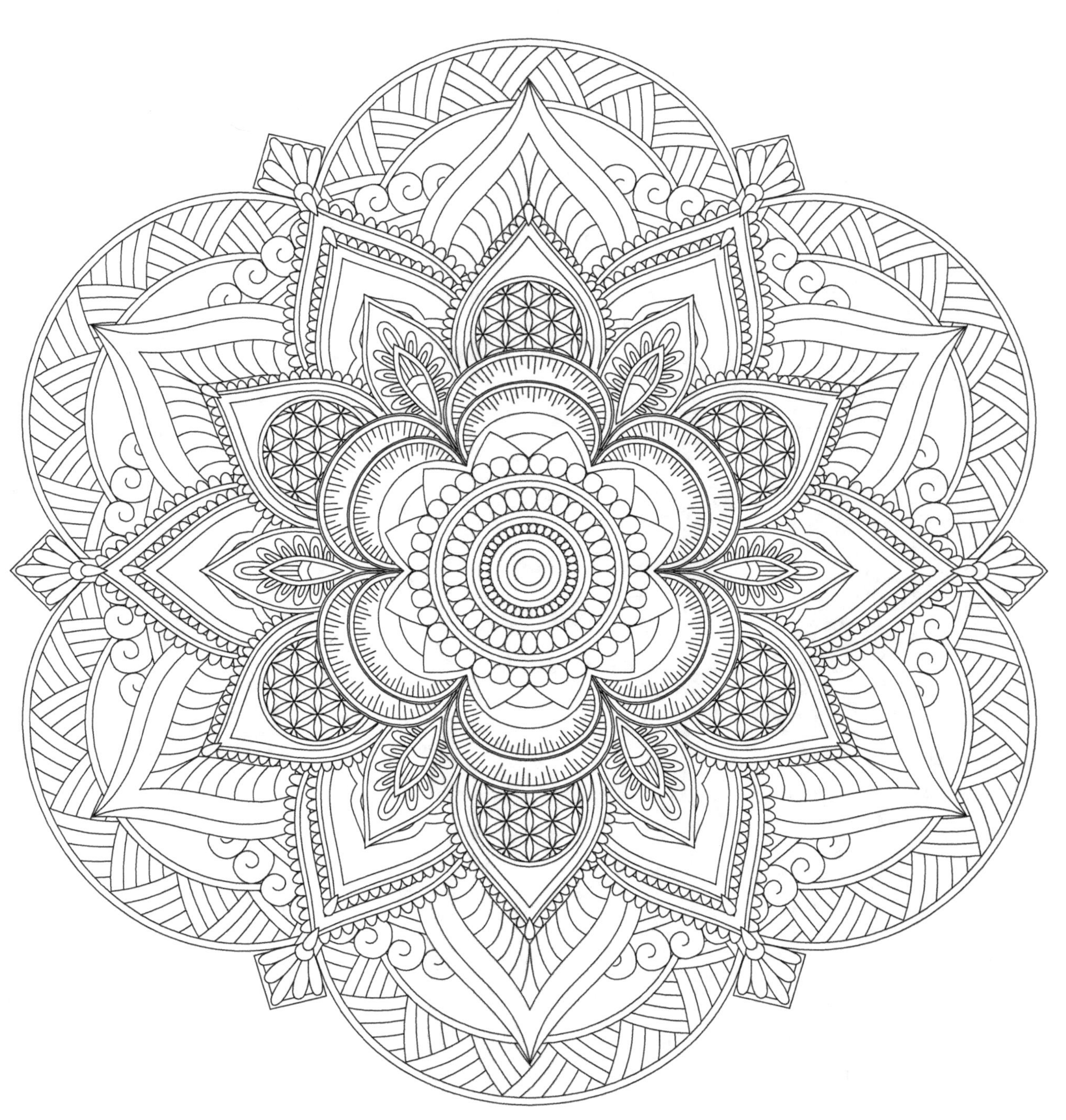

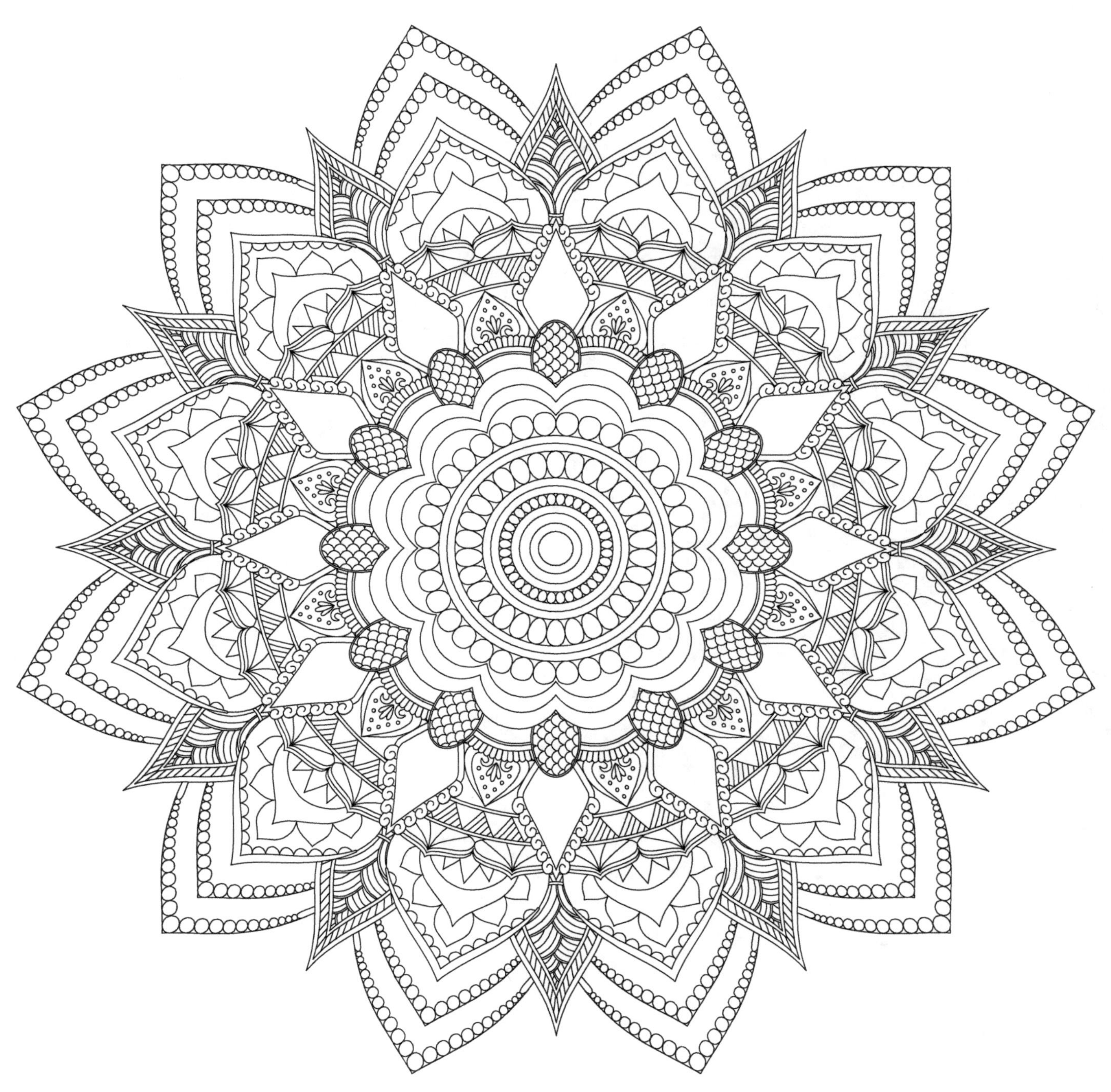

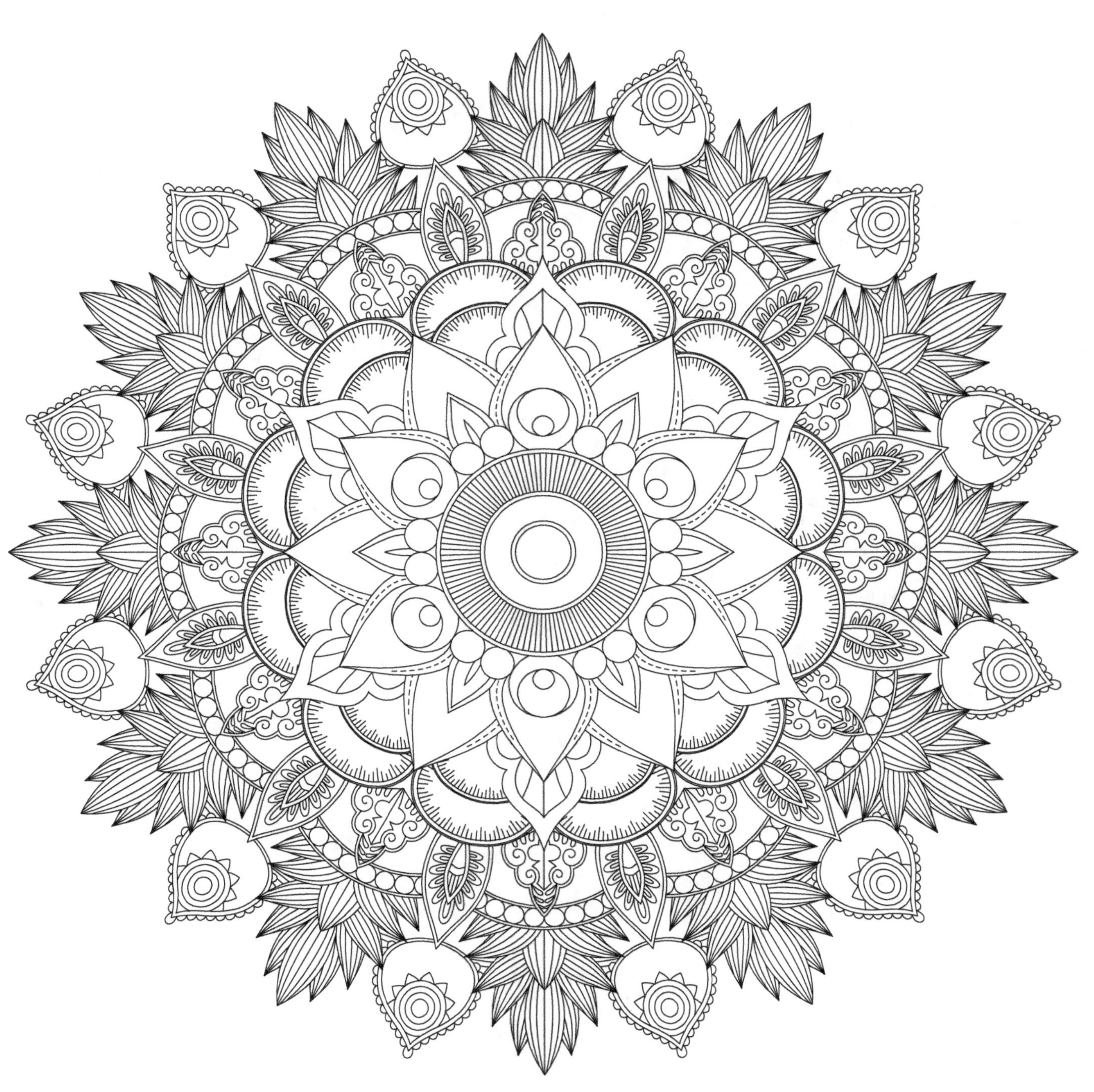

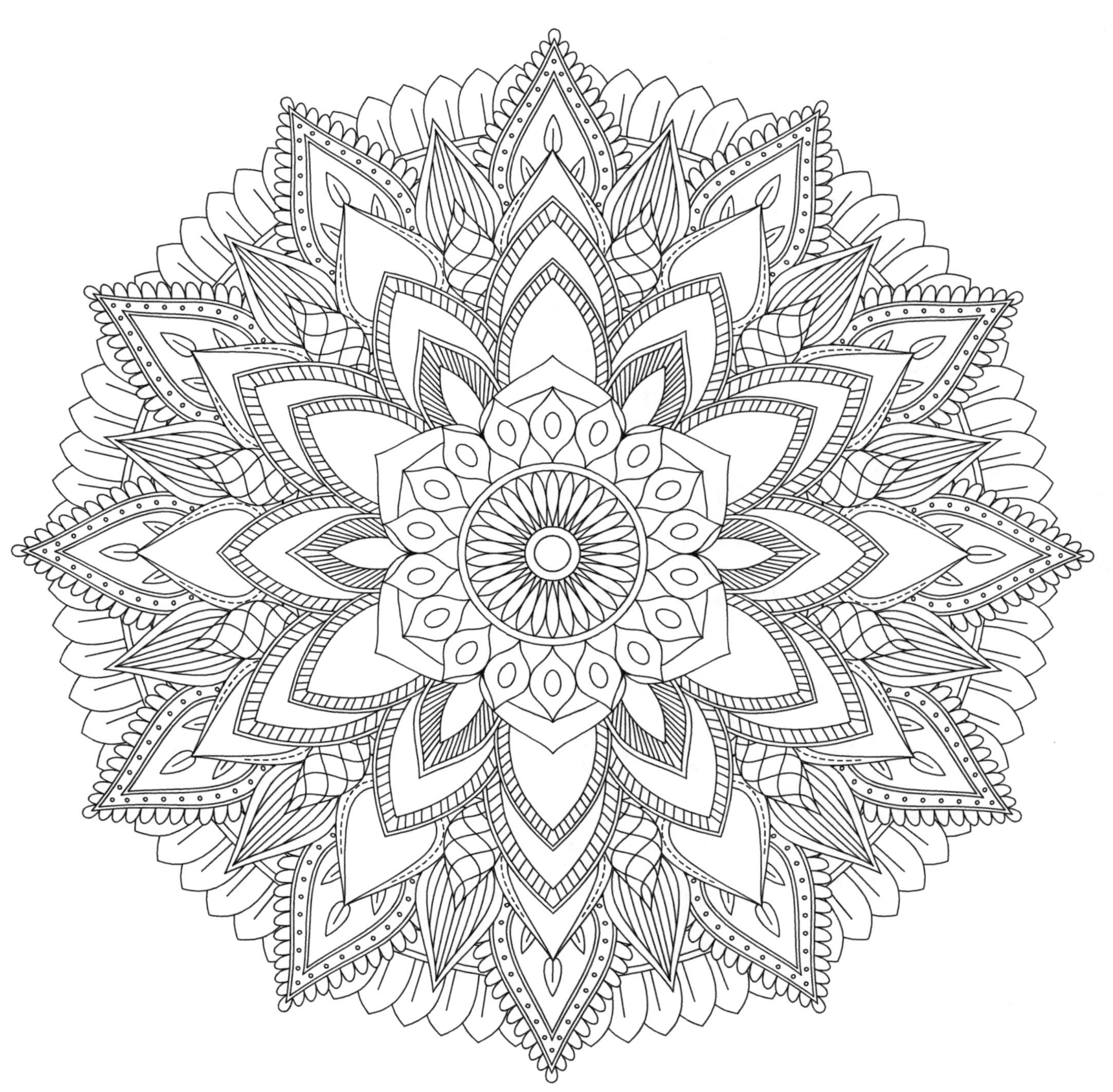

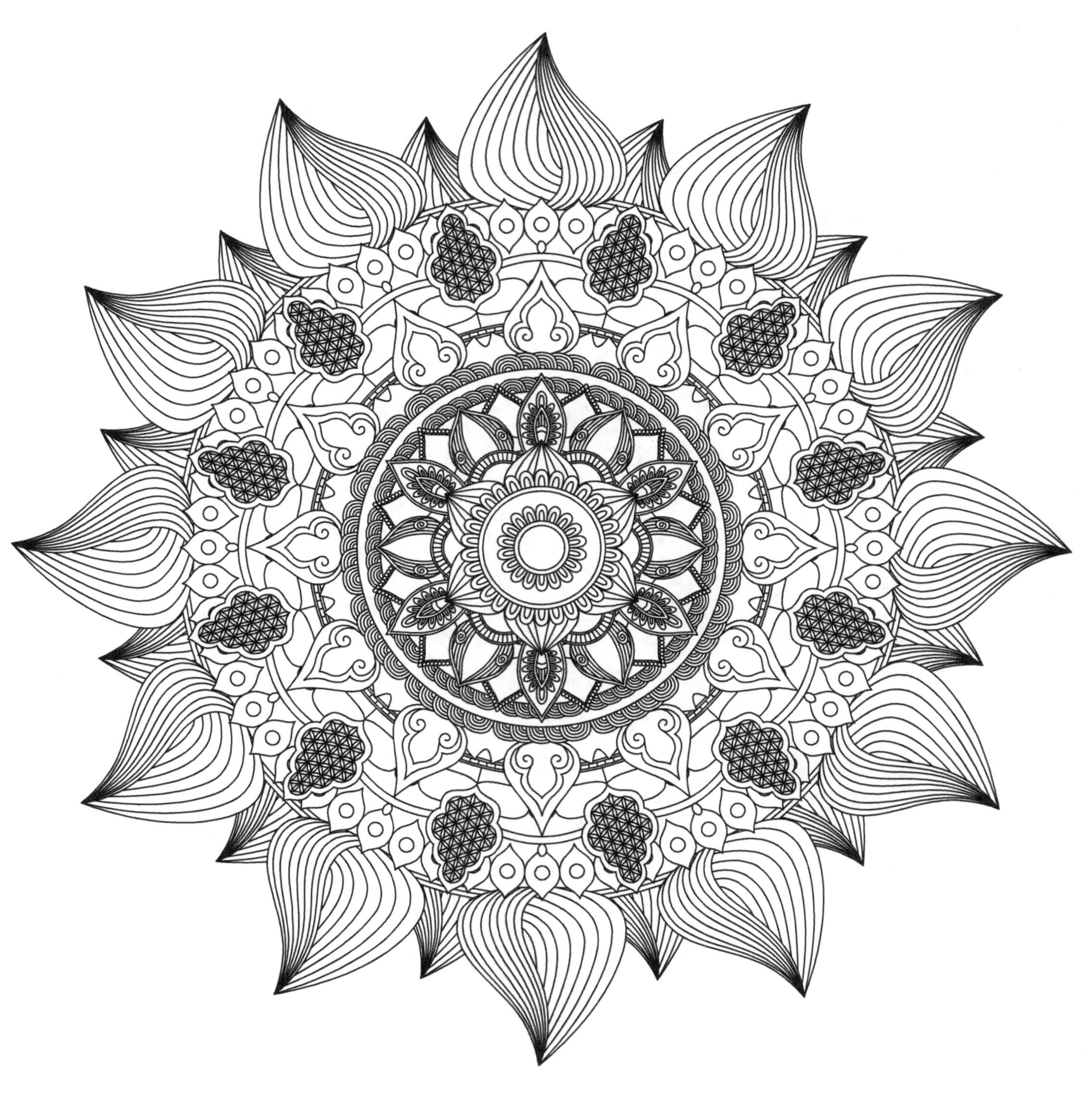

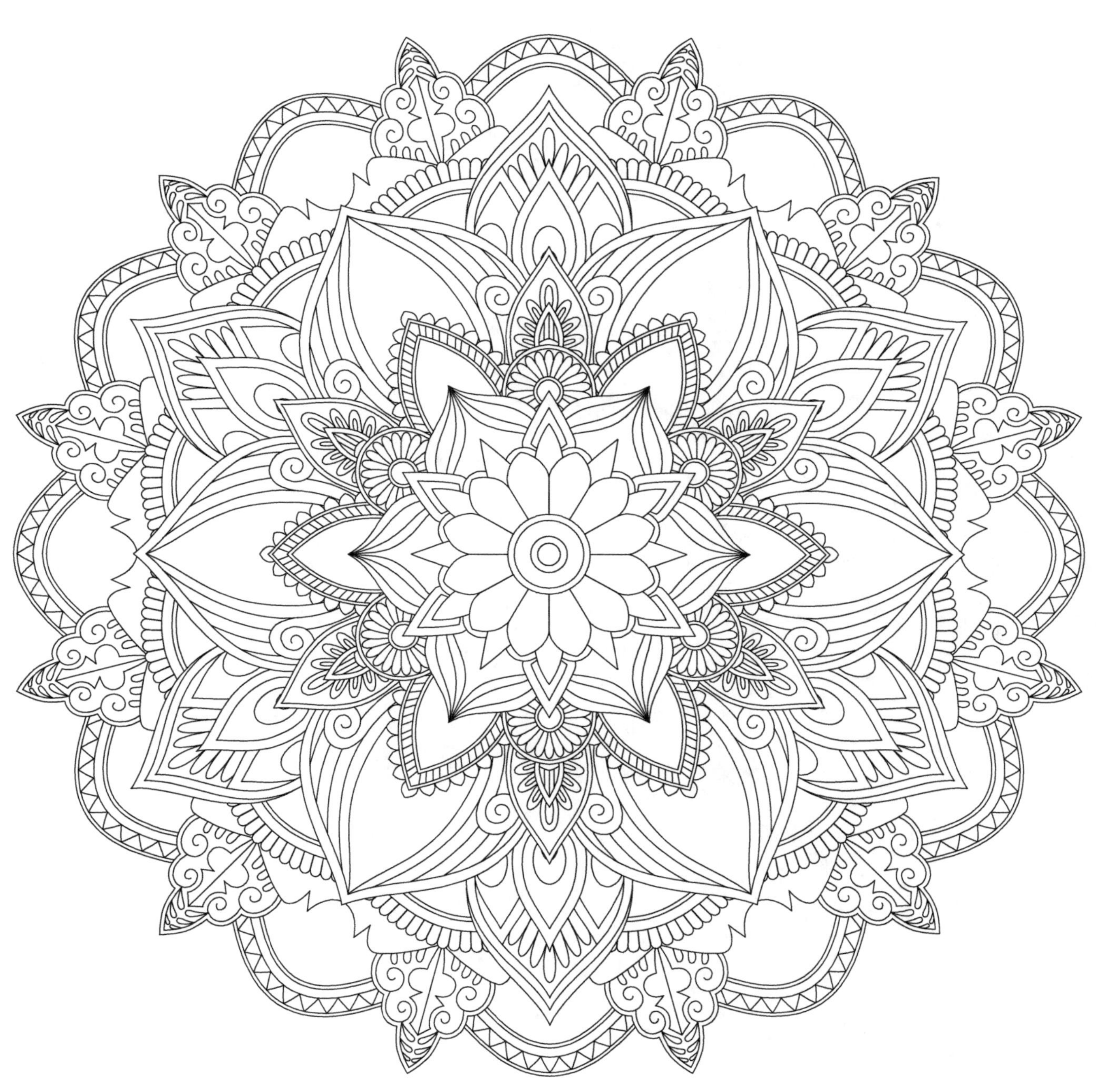

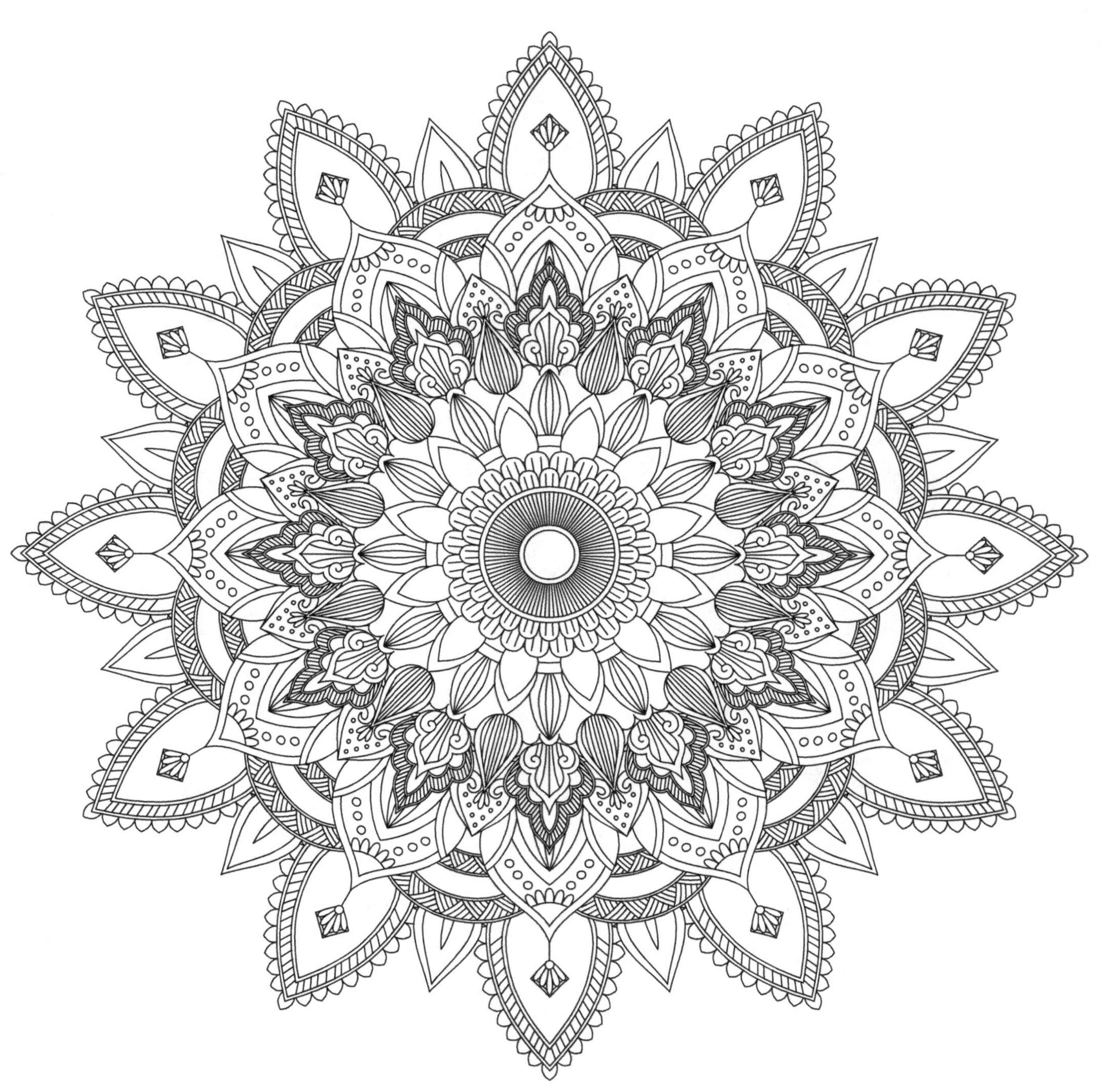

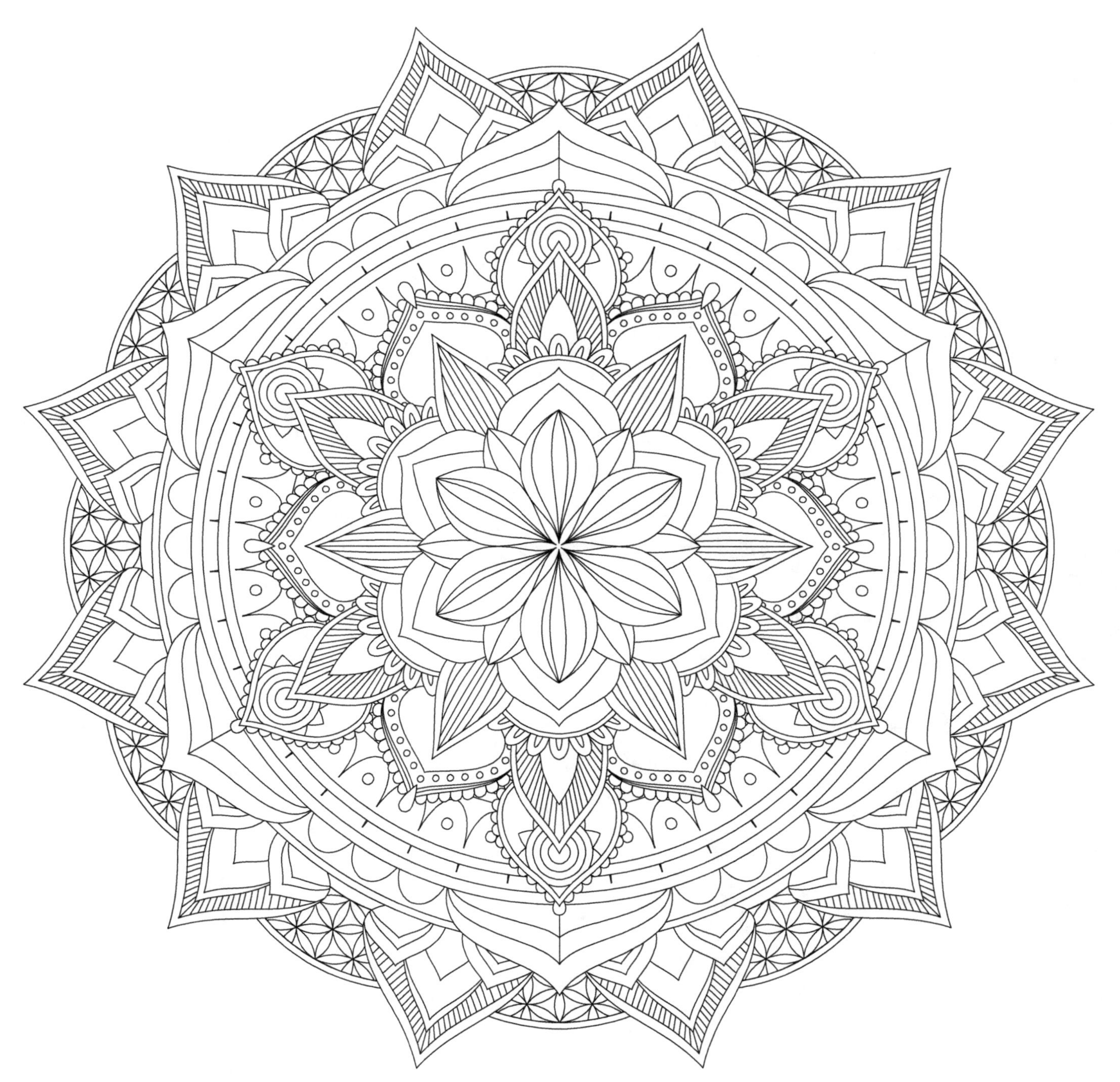

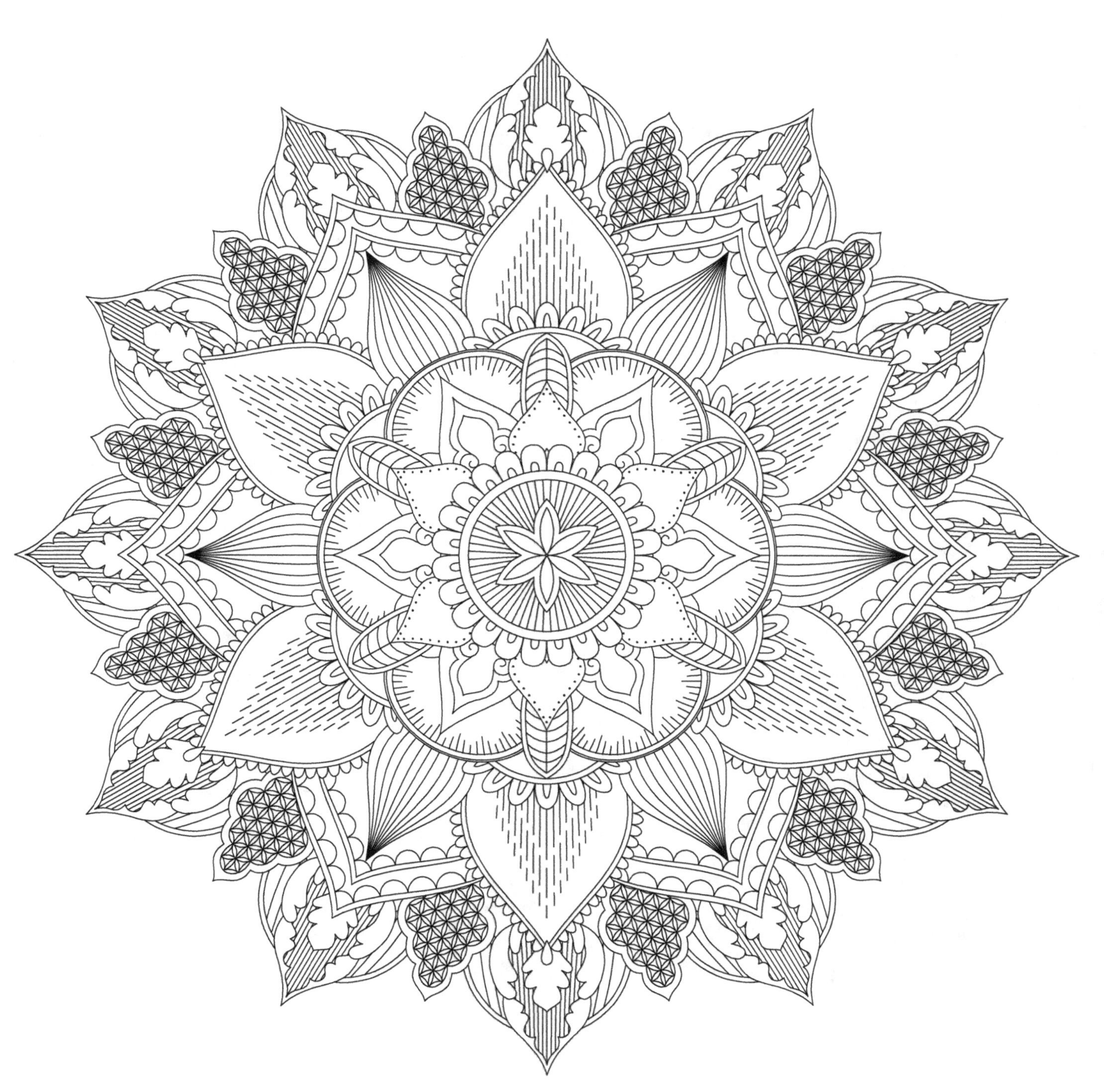

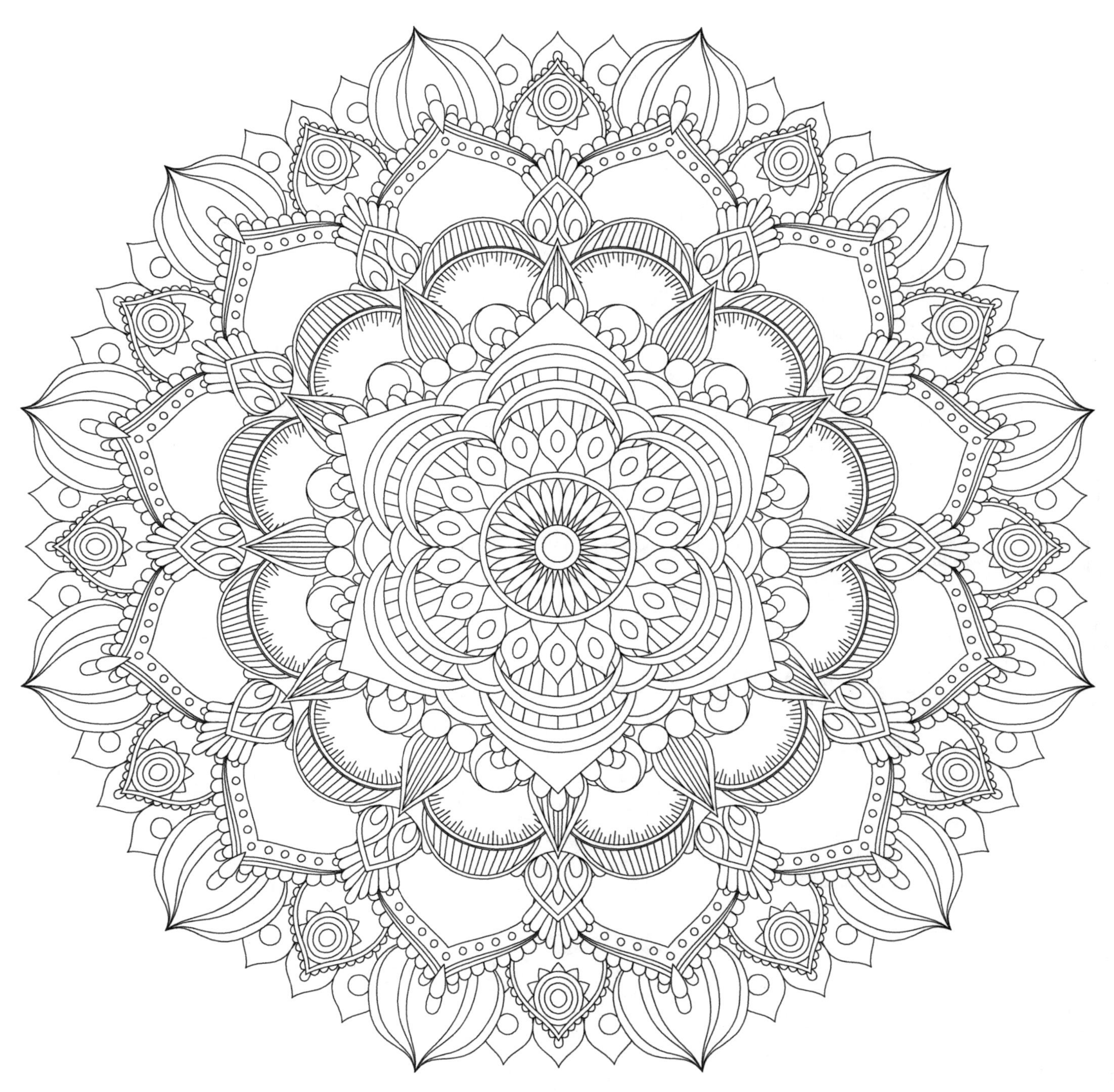